P9-BYQ-573

LEE TAKES COMMAND
From Seven Days to Second Bull Run

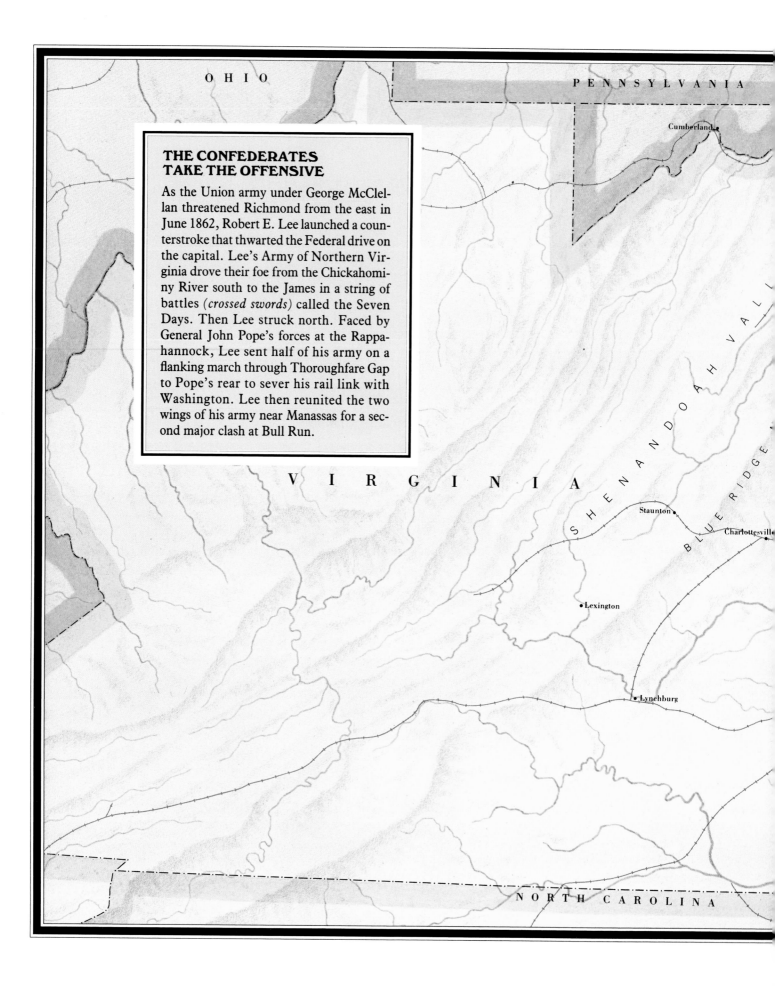

OHIO

PENNSYLVANIA

Cumberland

THE CONFEDERATES TAKE THE OFFENSIVE

As the Union army under George McClellan threatened Richmond from the east in June 1862, Robert E. Lee launched a counterstroke that thwarted the Federal drive on the capital. Lee's Army of Northern Virginia drove their foe from the Chickahominy River south to the James in a string of battles *(crossed swords)* called the Seven Days. Then Lee struck north. Faced by General John Pope's forces at the Rappahannock, Lee sent half of his army on a flanking march through Thoroughfare Gap to Pope's rear to sever his rail link with Washington. Lee then reunited the two wings of his army near Manassas for a second major clash at Bull Run.

VIRGINIA

SHENANDOAH VALLEY

BLUE RIDGE

Staunton

Charlottesville

Lexington

Lynchburg

NORTH CAROLINA

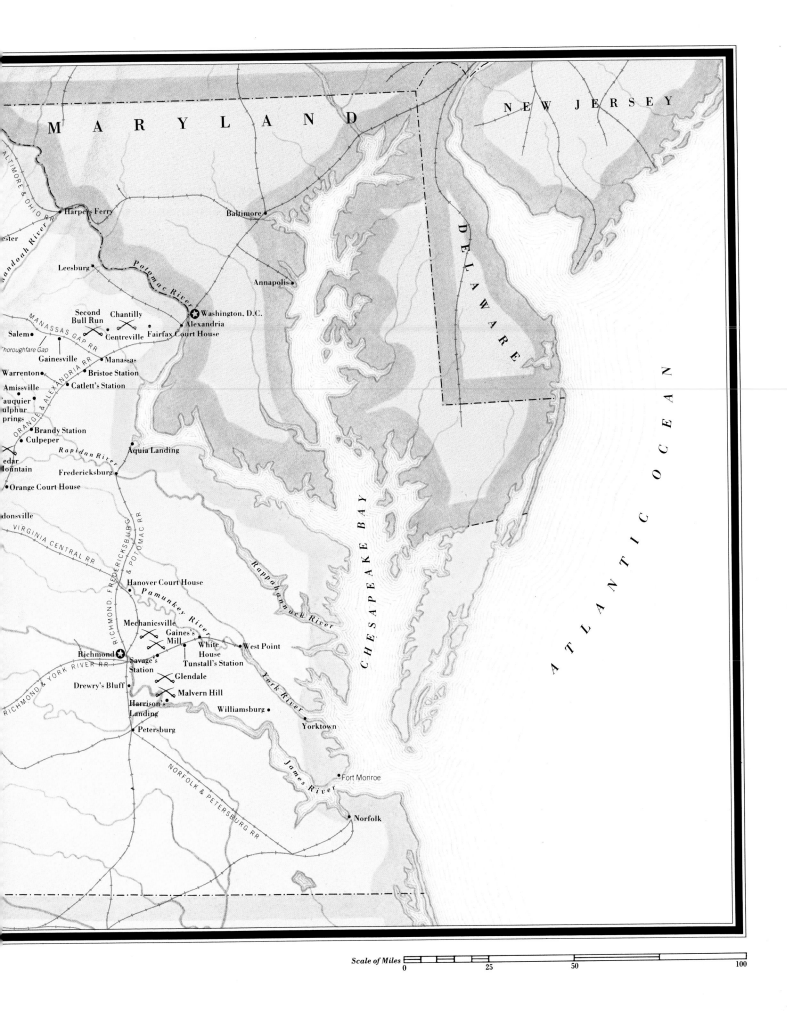

MARYLAND

NEW JERSEY

DELAWARE

ATLANTIC OCEAN

CHESAPEAKE BAY

BALTIMORE & OHIO RR

Harper's Ferry

Winchester

Shenandoah River

Leesburg

Potomac River

Baltimore

Annapolis

Second
Bull Run

Chantilly

Washington, D.C.

Alexandria

Salem

MANASSAS GAP RR

Centreville

Fairfax Court House

Thoroughfare Gap

Gainesville

Manassas

ORANGE & ALEXANDRIA RR

Warrenton

Bristoe Station

Amissville

Catlett's Station

Fauquier
Sulphur
Springs

Brandy Station

Culpeper

Rapidan River

Aquia Landing

Cedar
Mountain

Fredericksburg

Orange Court House

Gordonsville

VIRGINIA CENTRAL RR

RICHMOND, FREDERICKSBURG & POTOMAC RR

Rappahannock River

Hanover Court House

Pamunkey River

Mechanicsville

Gaines's
Mill

White
House

West Point

Richmond

Savage's
Station

Tunstall's Station

York River

RICHMOND & YORK RIVER RR

Drewry's Bluff

Glendale

Malvern Hill

Harrison's
Landing

Williamsburg

Yorktown

Petersburg

James River

NORFOLK & PETERSBURG RR

Fort Monroe

Norfolk

Scale of Miles

0   25   50   100

Other Publications:

UNDERSTANDING COMPUTERS
YOUR HOME
THE ENCHANTED WORLD
THE KODAK LIBRARY OF CREATIVE PHOTOGRAPHY
GREAT MEALS IN MINUTES
PLANET EARTH
COLLECTOR'S LIBRARY OF THE CIVIL WAR
THE EPIC OF FLIGHT
THE GOOD COOK
WORLD WAR II
HOME REPAIR AND IMPROVEMENT
THE OLD WEST

For information on and a full description of any of the
Time-Life Books series listed above, please write:
Reader Information, Time-Life Books
541 North Fairbanks Court, Chicago, Illinois 60611

This volume is one of a series that chronicles in full the
events of the American Civil War, 1861-1865.
Other books in the series include:
Brother against Brother: The War Begins
First Blood: Fort Sumter to Bull Run
The Blockade: Runners and Raiders
The Road to Shiloh: Early Battles in the West
Forward to Richmond: McClellan's Peninsular Campaign
Decoying the Yanks: Jackson's Valley Campaign
Confederate Ordeal: The Southern Home Front

The Cover: Astride his gray mount Traveller,
General Robert E. Lee pauses beneath an oak tree
with his senior officers to reconnoiter an enemy
position. The aggressive strategy Lee embraced after
taking command of the Army of Northern Virginia
reversed for a time the tide of the war in the East.

THE
CIVIL
WAR

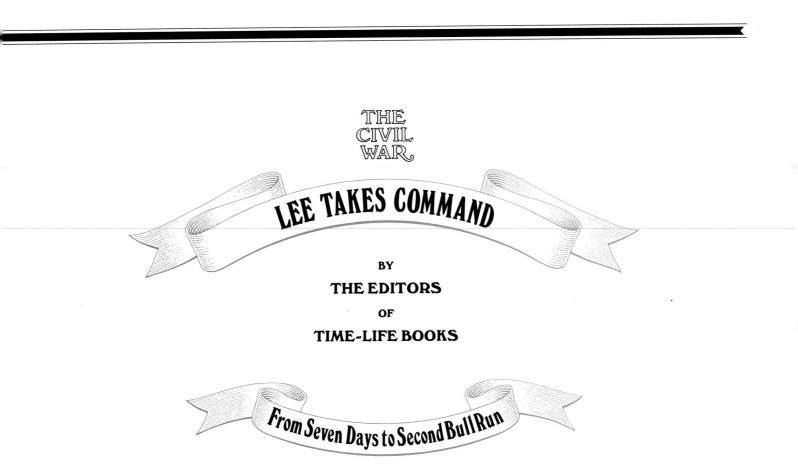

LEE TAKES COMMAND

BY

THE EDITORS

OF

TIME-LIFE BOOKS

From Seven Days to Second Bull Run

TIME-LIFE BOOKS, ALEXANDRIA, VIRGINIA

Time-Life Books Inc.
is a wholly owned subsidiary of

TIME INCORPORATED

FOUNDER: Henry R. Luce 1898-1967

Editor-in-Chief: Henry Anatole Grunwald
President: J. Richard Munro
Chairman of the Board: Ralph P. Davidson
Corporate Editor: Ray Cave
Group Vice President, Books: Reginald K. Brack Jr.
Vice President, Books: George Artandi

TIME-LIFE BOOKS INC.

EDITOR: George Constable
Executive Editor: George Daniels
Editorial General Manager: Neal Goff
Director of Design: Louis Klein
Director of Editorial Resources: Phyllis K. Wise
Editorial Board: Dale M. Brown, Roberta Conlan,
Ellen Phillips, Gerry Schremp, Donia Ann Steele,
Rosalind Stubenberg, Kit van Tulleken,
Henry Woodhead
Director of Research and Photography: John
Conrad Weiser

PRESIDENT: William J. Henry
Senior Vice President: Christopher T. Linen
Vice Presidents: Stephen L. Bair, Edward Brash,
Ralph J. Cuomo, Robert A. Ellis, John M. Fahey Jr.,
Juanita T. James, James L. Mercer, Wilhelm R. Saake,
Robert H. Smith, Paul R. Stewart, Leopoldo Toralballa

The Civil War

Series Director: Henry Woodhead
Designer: Herbert H. Quarmby
Series Administrator: Philip Brandt George

Editorial Staff for *Lee Takes Command*
Associate Editors: John Newton, Gerald Simons (text);
Jane N. Coughran (pictures)
Staff Writers: William C. Banks, Allan Fallow,
Adrienne George, David Johnson, Glenn McNatt
Researchers: Stephanie Lewis, Brian C. Pohanka
(principals); Harris J. Andrews
Assistant Designer: Cynthia T. Richardson
Copy Coordinator: Stephen G. Hyslop
Picture Coordinator: Betty H. Weatherley
Editorial Assistant: Andrea E. Reynolds
Special Contributors: Ronald Bailey, Jerry Korn,
David Nevin

Editorial Operations
Copy Chief: Diane Ullius
Editorial Operations: Caroline A. Boubin (manager)
Production: Celia Beattie
Quality Control: James J. Cox (director)
Library: Louise D. Forstall

Correspondents: Elisabeth Kraemer-Singh (Bonn);
Dorothy Bacon (London); Miriam Hsia (New York);
Maria Vincenza Aloisi, Josephine du Brusle (Paris); Ann
Natanson (Rome). Valuable assistance was also provided
by Carolyn Chubet (New York).

The Consultants:
Colonel John R. Elting, USA (Ret.), a former Associate
Professor at West Point, is the author of *Battles for Scandi-
navia* in the Time-Life Books World War II series and of
*The Battle of Bunker's Hill, The Battles of Saratoga, Mili-
tary History and Atlas of the Napoleonic Wars, American
Army Life* and *The Superstrategists.* Co-author of *A
Dictionary of Soldier Talk,* he is also editor of the three
volumes of *Military Uniforms in America, 1755-1867,* and
associate editor of *The West Point Atlas of American Wars.*

William A. Frassanito, a Civil War historian and lecturer
specializing in photograph analysis, is the author of two
award-winning studies, *Gettysburg: A Journey in Time* and
*Antietam: The Photographic Legacy of America's Bloodiest
Day,* and a companion volume, *Grant and Lee, The Virginia Campaigns.* He has also served as chief consultant to the
photographic history series *The Image of War.*

Les Jensen, Director of the Second Armored Division
Museum, Fort Hood, Texas, specializes in Civil War arti-
facts and is a conservator of historic flags. He is a contribu-
tor to *The Image of War* series, consultant for numerous
Civil War publications and museums, and a member of
the Company of Military Historians. He was formerly Curator of the U.S. Army Transportation Museum at Fort
Eustis, Virginia, and before that Curator of the Museum
of the Confederacy in Richmond, Virginia.

Michael McAfee specializes in military uniforms and has
been Curator of Uniforms and History at the West Point
Museum since 1970. A fellow of the Company of Military
Historians, he coedited with Colonel Elting *Long Endure:
The Civil War Years,* and he collaborated with Frederick
Todd on *American Military Equipage.* He has written nu-
merous articles for *Military Images Magazine,* as well as
Artillery of the American Revolution, 1775-1783.

© 1984 Time-Life Books Inc. All rights reserved.
No part of this book may be reproduced in any form or
by any electronic or mechanical means, including
information storage and retrieval devices or systems,
without prior written permission from the publisher,
except that brief passages may be quoted for reviews.
Second printing. Revised 1986. Printed in U.S.A.
Published simultaneously in Canada.
School and library distribution by Silver Burdett
Company, Morristown, New Jersey 07960.

TIME-LIFE is a trademark of Time Incorporated U.S.A.

Library of Congress Cataloguing in Publication Data
Main entry under title:
 Lee takes command.
 (The Civil War)
 Bibliography: p.
 Includes index.
  1. Peninsular Campaign, 1862. 2. Lee, Robert E.
(Robert Edward), 1807-1870. 3. Seven Days' Battle,
1862. 4. Cedar Mountain, Battle of, 1862. 5. Bull
Run, 2nd Battle, 1862.
I. Time-Life Books. II. Series.
E473.6.L45 1984   973.7'32   83-24382
ISBN 0-8094-4804-1
ISBN 0-8094-4805-X (lib. bdg.)

CONTENTS

The Making of a General

When General Robert E. Lee took command of the Confederate forces defending Richmond in June of 1862, he was famous yet little known. His family was celebrated in Virginia lore and American history, and his own brilliance during the invasion of Mexico in 1846 had won him a reputation as the most promising soldier of his generation. But Lee was puzzling — a man of iron self-control who revealed little of his innermost thoughts. Even his close friends agreed with Mary Chesnut, Southern diarist and social gadfly, who thought that Lee was strangely "cold and quiet and grand."

Yet despite his enigmatic reserve, Lee was quite understandable. There was, to begin with, a transparent logic to his choice of a military career. One of his ancestors had fought beside William the Conqueror; another had campaigned through the Holy Land in the Third Crusade; yet another had been knighted by Queen Elizabeth. Lee was brought up to be a gentleman soldier. As a grown man, he was widely considered the spiritual heir to George Washington, and some associates thought he consciously acted out the role. "General Lee," the Governor of Virginia once twitted him, "you certainly play Washington to perfection."

In fact, Lee made no bones about his strong sense of *noblesse oblige*. He once said: "There is a true glory and a true honor — the glory of duty done, the honor of the integrity of principle." In whatever service he rendered his countrymen, he was always kindly and courtly, with an almost saintly dedication to the right as he saw it. In short, he was a patrician, and so cool in manner that many thought he was cold. Yet beneath his aristocratic reserve beat a passionate heart. Lee was easily moved to tears and wept unabashedly on learning that a close comrade had been killed. When anger broke through his façade of studied calm, his neck turned red and his head jerked spasmodically, and those who had seen his rage before quickly departed the scene.

How Lee's background and training prepared him for his supreme trial is shown on the following pages. These early experiences put a sharp edge on his native military genius. He was uncanny in judging his opponent's strengths and weaknesses, and in turning both to his advantage. Perhaps his greatest asset was pure audacity — his willingness to run risks, his eagerness to attack, his instinct for taking the initiative at just the right moment.

All of Lee's assets came together and vaulted him to the peak of his profession in just three months — the time between his elevation to field command and the smashing victory he won in the second battle at Bull Run. With that triumph in August of 1862, Lee was well on his way to becoming the greatest soldier of the Civil War.

A powerful man nearly six feet tall, Robert E. Lee was soft-spoken, polite and even diffident. On the field of battle, his manner changed. "No man who saw his flashing eyes and sternly set lips," said an observer, "is ever likely to forget them."

An Austere Heritage

Robert E. Lee was born in 1807 at Stratford Hall (*opposite*), on the lower Potomac. Two years later, the Virginia estate passed by inheritance to his half brother. Soon after, Lee's spendthrift father, Henry "Light-Horse Harry" Lee, took the family to more modest quarters in Alexandria (*below*). When Robert was six, his father sought refuge in Barbados from his debts; Lee never saw him again. Thenceforth his mother, an invalid, determined to instill in Lee her code of self-control, frugality and honor.

Lee made her code his own and devoted countless hours to caring for her. When he left for West Point in 1825, she lamented: "How can I live without Robert? He is both son and daughter to me."

HENRY "LIGHT-HORSE HARRY" LEE   ANN HILL CARTER LEE

Alexandria was a bustling Potomac River port in 1811 when the Lee family moved into the light-colored house at left and a portion of the red brick buildin

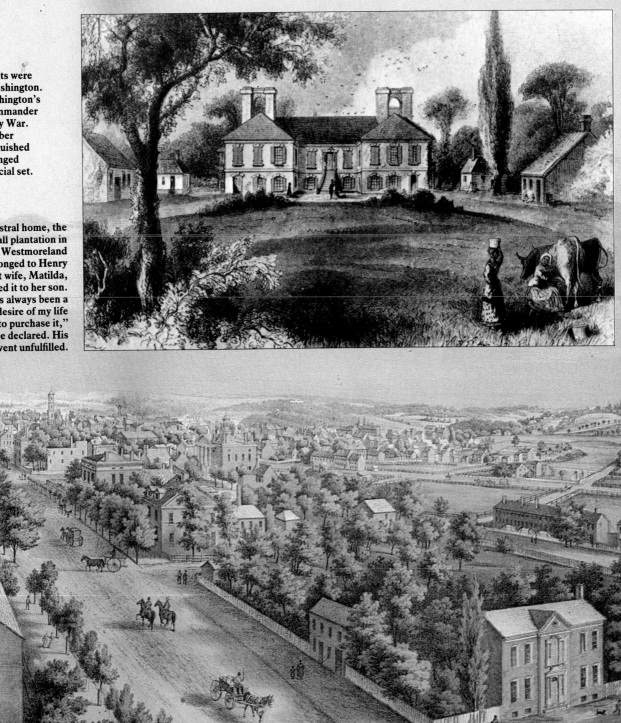

oth of Lee's parents were
ose to George Washington.
is father was Washington's
vorite cavalry commander
the Revolutionary War.
is mother, a member
Virginia's distinguished
arter family, belonged
Washington's social set.

Lee's ancestral home, the
Stratford Hall plantation in
Virginia's Westmoreland
County, belonged to Henry
Lee's first wife, Matilda,
who willed it to her son.
"It has always been a
great desire of my life
to be able to purchase it,"
Lee once declared. His
wish went unfulfilled.

adjoining it. Young Lee attended nearby Hallowell School, whose headmaster said he "imparted a finish and a neatness to everything he undertook."

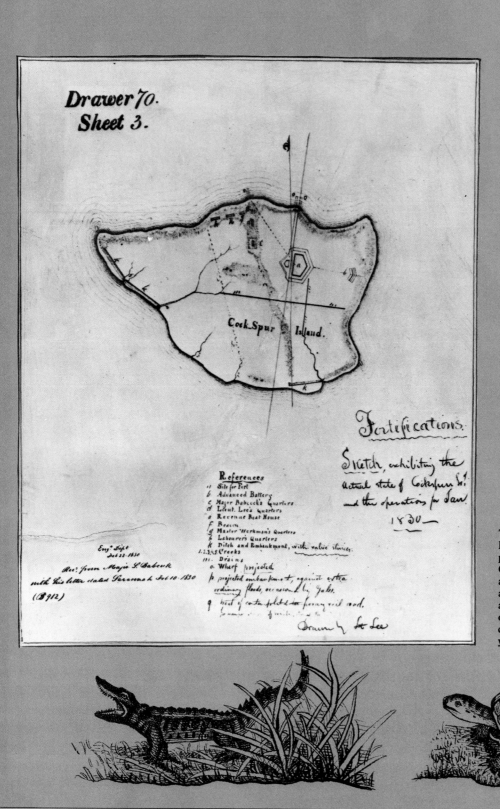

The Young Lieutenant at Work and Play

Lee's high standing as a graduate of West Point in 1829 — second in his class, and without a single demerit — qualified him for the top-rated branch of service, the Corps of Engineers. His first assignment, however, was hardly desirable. He reported to Cockspur Island, Georgia, off the mosquito-ridden coast at the mouth of the Savannah River. There Lee worked all day in waist-deep mud, building dikes and a drainage canal for the post that became Fort Pulaski.

All was not toil, though. In his off-duty hours Lee wrote letters, sketched, played cards or chess, and showed a vigorous interest in young women. Calling at the Savannah home of a West Point classmate, he regaled his friend's four sisters with lighthearted stories and flirtatious small talk. To one of the sisters, Lee later confided: "I have not had the heart to go to Savannah since you left it."

This diagram, made by Lee in 1830, shows the progress of fortifications at Cockspur Island. Lee was also gifted at drawing animals. He presented pen-and-ink sketches (*below*) of an alligator and a diamondback terrapin to a young woman in Savannah.

Clad in the dress uniform of a lieutenant of engineers, 31-year-old Robert E. Lee radiates confidence in his earliest known portrait, painted in 1838 by William E. West. Lee's wife pronounced the picture "a very admirable likeness."

Lee and his wife, Mary *(right)*, made their home in her parents' estate *(below)* in Arlington, Virginia. "Her thoughts were ever in the past at Arlington," said their youngest child, Mildred *(bottom right)*. Youngest son Robert Jr. *(far right)*, who later served under Stonewall Jackson, remembered his father always "romping, playing and joking with us."

Duty versus Domesticity

In June of 1831, Lee wed a distant cousin, Mary Custis, whose father was a grandson of Martha Washington and the adopted son of George Washington. The brilliant marriage was soon visited by misfortune: After giving birth to a second child in 1835, Mary was struck by arthritis. Lee was stunned. Said a relative, "I never saw a man so changed and saddened."

Despite her disability, Mary bore him five more children. Lee adored the youngsters. "The dearest annuals of the season," he called them. "I find something in every edition that I in vain look for elsewhere." Yet his love for the children made even more painful his long absences from his family on tours of duty in Texas and other distant places. Soldiering, he once complained, was a profession that "debars all hope of domestic enjoyment."

Eight-year-old Rooney (William Henry Fitzhugh Lee), who grew up to become a Confederate general, leans on his father's shoulder in a daguerreotype made around 1845. Lee found Rooney the most unruly of his three sons, complaining to his wife, "He seems only to have time or thought for running about."

Custis (George Washington Custis Lee), the oldest Lee child, appears in his cadet uniform at the time of his graduation from West Point in 1854. Though all of Lee's sons served in the Confederate Army during the Civil War, Custis was the only one who took soldiering for a career. Like his brother Rooney, he rose to the rank of general.

In one of the first war photographs, General John Wool *(left of center)* leads officers through Saltillo, Mexico, in 1847. Lee, who built roads and bridges for Wool, is thought to be among the group.

The Mexican War Hero

Lee's first taste of fighting came during the Mexican War, and he distinguished himself. In the course of the American bombardment of Veracruz *(right)*, the young captain emplaced a six-gun battery that pummeled the stronghold with 1,800 rounds and forced it to surrender.

At Cerro Gordo, Lee guided a brigade behind the Mexican line, forcing the enemy to retreat. Near Mexico City, he helped outflank the foe by finding a path through a jagged lava field that was believed impenetrable. Lee was thrice brevetted, and General Winfield Scott, the U.S. commander, called him "the very best soldier that I ever saw in the field."

A shell fired from the walled city of Veracruz explodes amid a battery of U.S. guns. Lee had brought the

Lee sports a mustache in a photograph taken shortly after the end of the Mexican War. Later, the military collar was etched in over Lee's civilian dress.

guns ashore and emplaced them only 700 yards from the walls, pinning down the Mexican defenders within the stronghold.

VIEW OF WEST POINT,
UNITED STATES MILITARY ACADEMY.

Commandant at the School for Soldiers

When Robert E. Lee received orders naming him the Superintendent of West Point in 1852, he greeted the news "with much regret." In a letter to the Secretary of War, Lee sought to avoid the appointment, claiming that the post required "more skill and more experience than I command."

Once his appeal was denied, Lee launched into his new duty with tireless zeal. He erected stables for the horses and expanded the officers' quarters and the cadet hospital. He tightened discipline and raised academic standards.

For all these improvements, Lee was best remembered by the cadets for his stately bearing. William Averell, who later would fight Lee's Confederates outside Richmond, wrote: "His unaffected natural dignity and grace of manner presented a personal equilibrium which nothing could disturb."

Lee's engraved .28-caliber revolver was given to him by arms manufacturer Samuel Colt at the end of his tenure at West Point. The gun's perfect condition suggests that Lee rarely used it.

est Point presents a
esh aspect in this 1856
thograph, made after
e three-year term of
e academy's ninth
perintendent, Robert E.
ee. Among the new
ructures were a cadet
arracks *(top left)* and a
ding hall *(right).*

This portrait of Lee, by
West Point professor and
artist Robert Weir, was
unpopular with the Lees.
Declared his son Robert,
"The strength peculiar
to his face is wanting."

Flushing out John Brown and his men, U.S. Marines under Lieutenant Colonel Lee stave in the doors of the U.S. Armory's engine house at Harpers Ferry

The Die Is Cast

Lee shunned politics before the War, even as his duties thrust him into the center of controversy between North and South. In October of 1859, he led 93 U.S. Marines to Harpers Ferry (*above*), where they crushed John Brown's effort to start a slave rebellion. As usual, Lee was conscientious, protecting the captured abolitionists from mob violence.

But soon he was forced to choose sides. In early 1861, after the Confederacy had been formed, Lee was called to Washington and discreetly offered the field command of a new army being raised to suppress the rebellion. Lee refused the post, explaining that as a loyal Virginian, "I could take no part in an invasion of the Southern States."

Arlington, Washington City P.O.
20 April 1861

Hon.ᵇˡᵉ Simon Cameron
Sec.ᵗ of War

Sir
I have the honour to tender the resignation of my Commission as Colonel of the 1st Reg.ᵗ of Cavalry
very resp.ᵗ your Obt.ᵗ
R E Lee
Col 1.ˢᵗ Cav.ʸ

Lee penned his resignation from the U.S. Army shortly after learning that his native Virginia had seceded

This 1862 photograph of Robert E. Lee was the first picture of him taken after the War began. Lee had recently grown his wiry white beard, which, he told his daughter, "is much admired."

Mechanicsville to Gaines's Mill

"The valley was filled with an impenetrable smoke and nothing could be seen but the fire belching from the guns. Loud above all was the exultant, fiendlike yell of the Confederate soldiers."

PRIVATE THOMAS SOUTHWICK, 5TH NEW YORK, AT GAINES'S MILL

1

Few cheers greeted the selection of Robert Edward Lee to command the Confederate army defending Richmond in the early summer of 1862. The man he replaced, General Joseph E. Johnston, was a genuine Confederate hero; and many anxious Southerners believed the shell that had wounded Johnston at the Battle of Seven Pines had dealt the South an almost irreparable injury.

The Richmond *Examiner* described the new commander scathingly as "a general who had never fought a battle, who had a pious horror of guerrillas, and whose extreme tenderness of blood inclined him to depend exclusively on the resources of strategy." The Richmond *Whig* was less hostile, but it reported hearing much "disparagement, sarcasm and ridicule" of Lee. The general's own new subordinates muttered uneasily that they were now being led by a staff officer who had never shown that he had the "power and skill for field service."

It was Joseph Johnston, after all, who had created the army protecting the capital, and there was a feeling that no one else had the right—or the brilliance—to lead it.

Even the enemy commander concurred in the view that Lee was Johnston's inferior. Major General George B. McClellan, in charge of the Federal troops pressing close to Richmond, had known both men well during the Mexican War, and he professed delight at the change of command. "I prefer Lee to Johnston," he wrote. "The former is too cautious and weak under grave responsi-

bility—personally brave and energetic to a fault, he yet is wanting in moral firmness when pressed by heavy responsibility and is likely to be timid and irresolute in action."

Much of the criticism of Lee in the South arose from the fact that a great deal had been expected of him, and it was widely felt that he had failed to live up to his promise. At the outbreak of war, when Lee resigned from the U.S. Army, he had been one of the nation's best-known soldiers. In the year since then, all had somehow been anticlimactic. A Virginian, Lee had accepted command of his state's troops, but as far as most Southerners could tell, he had had little influence on the course of the War. Charged with preserving Union-leaning western Virginia for the Confederacy, he had evolved a bold but complicated plan for defeating the Federals there. It had miscarried, in part because Lee was ill served by his subordinates, and in September 1861 the Confederate troops withdrew after a defeat at Cheat Mountain.

When Lee returned to Richmond after this frustrating venture, some Southern newspapers called him "Evacuating Lee." He was also known—for his gray hair and for what some considered his fussiness—as "Granny Lee."

Lee's setback in western Virginia was followed by what he described as "another forlorn expedition," supervising the building of fortifications along the coasts of South Carolina and Georgia. Next came the equally thankless job of military adviser to President

General George B. McClellan, commander of the Army of the Potomac during the Peninsular Campaign, was a former railroad executive with a gift for military administration. However, Lincoln found him sadly lacking in fighting spirit, and complained: "McClellan is a great engineer, but he has a special talent for a stationary engine."

Jefferson Davis. Lee performed masterfully in this position, launching Stonewall Jackson's brilliant campaign in the Shenandoah Valley and arranging for Joseph Johnston's month-long defense of the Yorktown line on the Peninsula below Richmond. But few outside the government knew of these behind-the-scenes efforts. Robert E. Lee seemed to be just one more big name from the prewar Army who had not panned out.

But there were dissenters from this view, and if their voices were not very audible above the clamor in June 1862, they would be remembered later.

One man who appreciated Lee's talents was Colonel Joseph Ives, who had known the general in South Carolina. Ives was riding that June among Richmond's defenses when a fellow officer, Major E. Porter Alexander, asked him a crucial question: "Ives, tell me this. We are here fortifying our lines, but apparently leaving the enemy all the time he needs to accumulate his superior forces and then to move on us in the way he thinks best. Has General Lee the audacity that is going to be required for our inferior force to meet the enemy's superior force — to take the aggressive and to run risks and stand chances?"

Ives stopped his mount and faced the other man. "Alexander," he said, "if there is one man in either army, Confederate or Federal, head and shoulders above every other in audacity, it is General Lee! His name might be Audacity. He will take more desperate chances, and take them quicker, than any other general in this country, North or South; and you will live to see it, too."

Another dissenter was Joseph Johnston. He had had his differences with Lee in the past, but when a friend suggested that his wounds spelled disaster for the Confederate

cause, Johnston replied sharply: "No, Sir! The shot that struck me down is the very best that has been fired for the Southern cause yet. For I possess in no degree the confidence of our government, and now they have in my place one who does possess it, and who can accomplish what I never could have done — the concentration of our armies for the defense of the capital of the Confederacy."

Whoever was to be in charge, the task appeared formidable. There were about 50,000 Confederate troops arrayed outside the Confederate capital. Although full of fight, they were poorly disciplined and not very well cared for; one soldier complained that their bacon was strong, their bread sour and their trousers threadbare in the seat. Facing them was a magnificently equipped and superbly trained force of 100,000 Federals. The 2-to-1 mathematics of the situation seemed inescapable: Once the Federal army launched its onslaught, Richmond must fall.

But time passed and the gargantuan Federal force remained frozen in place astride the Chickahominy River, two corps on the north bank and three to the south. George McClellan had brought his mighty army a long distance and had planned very carefully; he did not want things to go wrong now. From the outset his pace had been deliberate. It had been three months since his troops had landed at Fort Monroe, 100 miles from Richmond, to begin their advance up the Peninsula. The battle outside the Confederate capital near the hamlet of Seven Pines had cost McClellan 5,000 casualties. Although the Confederates had lost 6,000 men, they had very nearly won a victory. More important, the blood bath had sobered — and intimidated — McClellan. On June 2, the day after the battle, he wrote his wife, "I feel sure of success, so good is the spirit of my men and so great their ardor. But I am tired of the battle-field, with its mangled corpses and poor wounded. Victory has no charms for me when purchased at such cost."

McClellan hesitated. It rained virtually every day for a fortnight; he needed time to rebuild his 11 bridges over the raging Chickahominy and time, too, for the roads to harden so he could move up his big guns. All the while McClellan kept up his demands that Major General Irvin McDowell's 30,000-man Army of the Rappahannock be sent south to join him. For a time it seemed that the government would comply; but the threat posed by Stonewall Jackson's army in the Shenandoah Valley permitted only one of McDowell's divisions to be shipped south.

Lee made good use of this precious time. He had inherited a loose-knit army — which he named the Army of Northern Virginia — composed of Johnston's Manassas veterans, the original Peninsula defense force under Major General John B. Magruder, and a hodgepodge of reinforcements now arriving from southern Virginia, South Carolina and Georgia. Lee tried to integrate these various forces and tighten the slackness that had characterized Johnston's command. He stressed discipline and sobriety (Lee himself would take nothing stronger than a little wine). He got better rations and uniforms for his troops. And he strengthened his officer corps, promoting deserving men and sacking incompetents.

Lee also tackled the attitude of defeatism among some of his generals who, at least until the near victory at Seven Pines, had grown dangerously accustomed to retreating.

Lee saw this clearly at his first meeting with his four dozen or so general officers. He found that a surprising number favored pulling back even farther upon the outskirts of Richmond. For example, Brigadier General William H. C. Whiting, a division commander and an excellent engineer, stepped forward to demonstrate mathematically the inevitability of McClellan's advance. As Whiting drew diagrams showing the Union's siege guns inching ever nearer to the capital, Lee watched with growing impatience. Finally, his forbearance snapped. "Stop! stop!" he exclaimed. "If we go to ciphering we shall be whipped beforehand."

Instead of withdrawing, Lee set about fortifying his position with earthworks — trenches, breastworks, redoubts. The Confederate line stretched for more than eight miles from White Oak Swamp north to New Bridge on the Chickahominy River. Then it curved northwestward along the near bank of the river to beyond the Mechanicsville bridges. Up and down the line, soldiers were set to work with pick and shovel. Many grumbled as they dug, and they began calling Lee by the name that the troops had given him in South Carolina: "King of Spades."

East of the Confederates, less than a mile away, the Federals manned a north-south line centered on the village of Fair Oaks. They too were at work with pick and shovel. McClellan intended to tighten his grip on Richmond through the kind of elaborate siegework he had studied in Europe. "I will bring up my heavy guns," he wrote, "shell the city, and carry it by assault."

Lee had correctly divined these intentions and was developing a strategy to foil them — one that involved more than building earthworks. On June 5 Lee set forth his ideas in a message to President Davis, whom he took

As a clean-shaven youth, J.E.B. (Jeb) Stuart had been so homely that his West Point classmates jokingly nicknamed him Beauty. But as the bearded commander of Robert E. Lee's cavalry, he cut a dashing figure in stylish trappings: a tasseled yellow sash, scarlet-lined cape and a gray felt hat topped with a foot-long ostrich plume.

care to consult with on a daily basis (as Johnston had not). "McClellan will make this a battle of posts," Lee wrote. "He will take position from position, under cover of his heavy guns. I am preparing a line that I can hold with part of our forces in front, while with the rest I will endeavour to make a diversion to bring McClellan out."

The diversion Lee had in mind was nothing less than a full-scale attack north of the Chickahominy. While part of his army held the new earthworks below the river east of Richmond, the rest would cross over the Chickahominy near Mechanicsville and strike McClellan's extended right wing on the north bank. Such a maneuver would threaten McClellan's supply line, which ran along the Richmond & York River Railroad from White House Landing on the Pamunkey River. The Confederate stroke would pry McClellan out of his entrenchments south of the Chickahominy and force him to fight in the open. Such an attack, Lee told Davis, would forestall McClellan's projected siege — and might actually "change the character of the war."

Before planning the details of the attack, Lee needed to know the precise dispositions of the Federal right wing north of the Chickahominy. The tip of this wing consisted of Brigadier General Fitz-John Porter's V Corps, which had initially been deployed to serve as a link with the long-promised and often-postponed march of Irvin McDowell's troops from Fredericksburg.

To map Porter's exact whereabouts, Lee ordered his cavalry chief, Brigadier General James Ewell Brown (Jeb) Stuart, to conduct a reconnaissance in force north of Richmond. Thus was set in motion one of the

The Burial of a Fallen Confederate

The only Confederate to lose his life during Jeb Stuart's sweep around the Federal army in June 1862 was 29-year-old Captain William Latané. He died in his brother's arms — and overnight became a Southern hero.

Latané was shot from his horse in a skirmish with Federal cavalry near Hanover Court House. His brother John, also a Confederate trooper, had the body carried to a nearby plantation. There the mistress and her sister-in-law, alone while their men were at war, held a simple funeral service and buried the slain captain in their family plot.

When news of Latané's death reached Richmond, poet John R. Thompson wrote an elegy honoring the fallen warrior. The poem inspired painter William D. Washington to re-create the graveside scene (*below*), using Richmond society women as models. Finished in 1864, the painting was widely reproduced throughout the South. At its first public showing in Richmond, a bucket was placed beneath the canvas to solicit contributions to the Confederate cause — and was quickly filled to overflowing.

William Washington's emotional *Burial of Latané* depicts the young officer's grave surrounded by bereaved women, children and household servants.

War's most dramatic cavalry expeditions.

The flamboyant Stuart welcomed the mission, sensing an opportunity for the derring-do on which he thrived. Only 29 years old, stockily built, with a thick, curled mustache and a wide-spreading reddish brown beard, Stuart was a storybook cavalryman.

On June 12 Stuart arose at 2 a.m. and ordered his troopers to be in the saddle in 10 minutes. He had selected 1,200 men from four regiments, plus two pieces of horse artillery. The force included two colonels with strikingly similar names: Fitzhugh Lee, a 26-year-old nephew of Robert E. Lee, and William Henry Fitzhugh Lee, known to everyone as Rooney, the 25-year-old second son of the new commanding general.

None of the troopers except Stuart knew where they were going. The half-mile-long column headed northwest out of Richmond to create the impression that it was merely a body of cavalry reinforcements being sent to Jackson up in the Shenandoah Valley.

The column crossed the headwaters of the Chickahominy, then turned sharply east and camped that night a few miles short of Hanover Court House. The next morning, Stuart flushed a handful of Federal cavalry pickets, then sliced southeastward on back roads. This route took him behind Porter's corps, on the flank of McClellan's right wing.

Early in the afternoon, a dozen or so miles down the road, Stuart's column ran head on into a detachment of the 5th U.S. Cavalry. Rooney Lee ordered a squadron of his 9th Virginia Cavalry to charge. Led by Captain William Latané, the Confederate troopers overwhelmed their opponents in a brief saber-swinging melee. But when the dust settled, Latané lay dead in the road — killed by the revolver shot of a Federal captain.

Stuart's men rode on a couple of miles to Old Church crossroads, looted and burned a lightly defended Federal cavalry camp, taking some prisoners, and then drew up. Here at Old Church, Stuart faced a decision. His roughly semicircular route from Richmond had taken him perhaps 35 miles — around and behind Porter's corps, and now to a point a few miles to the rear of Brigadier General William Franklin's VI Corps. Stuart was so deep in Federal-occupied territory that one of his men, looking southwest toward the Chickahominy, thought he could see McClellan's headquarters camp several miles in the distance.

It seemed to be time for Stuart's column to turn around and retrace its path to Richmond. Stuart had gathered all the information Lee wanted. But from the beginning of the mission, Stuart had harbored a wild and splendid notion: to ride all the way around McClellan's army.

Union forces would have been alerted by now, Stuart reasoned, and would likely be waiting in ambush if he returned by the same route. It would actually be safer — "the quintessence of prudence," he later reported — to ride on and circle McClellan.

Stuart signaled his column forward. Now began "the gayest portion of the ride," wrote staff Lieutenant John Esten Cooke, Stuart's brother-in-law. "It was neck or nothing." Cooke reckoned their chances of survival at 1 in 10.

That afternoon, however, the ride took on the trappings of a triumphal tour. Many of the troopers had homes in the area, and as they headed southeast, women poured from the houses to bring food and to embrace sons, brothers, husbands and sweethearts they had not seen since the War began.

By the time the column approached Tunstall's Station, on the Richmond & York River Railroad about nine miles southeast of Old Church, all were in grand spirits. With a great war cry, grayclad horsemen swooped down on the station, seized two squads of bewildered Federal guards and set about wrecking the place. They torched supply wagons and shot up a Federal supply train eastbound for White House Landing.

Stuart then led the column four miles to Talleysville, where he left unmolested a Union field hospital containing several hundred wounded, but allowed his men to refresh themselves with sausages, figs and other victuals from a sutler's store.

It was midnight before Stuart left Talleysville on the next perilous leg of the journey, to the lower Chickahominy seven miles to the south. The column was slowed by its burden of 165 Union prisoners — riding double on captured horses and mules — and by the troopers' own exhaustion. They had now spent more than two days in the saddle, and even the tireless Stuart was so weary he kept nodding off as he rode, his plumed hat dropping lower and lower.

The moon was dangerously bright, and the slow-moving Confederate horsemen expected Union cavalry to pounce upon them at any moment. Lieutenant W. W. Robins recalled that "every bush in the distance

Dismounted, Confederate troopers led by Brigadier General Jeb Stuart fire on a Federal supply train at Tunstall's Station during their daring ride around McClellan's army. The Federals were so startled by the attack that a paymaster leaped off the train, leaving $125,000 in cash behind. Fortunately for him, the train broke through the Confederate ambush and the money was secured.

A mile down the river, the Confederates discovered an old skiff and anchored it in the middle of the 40-foot-wide channel. Then, using the skiff for a pontoon, they attempted to bridge the channel with timbers salvaged from a nearby warehouse. When Stuart saw that the timbers would reach — just barely — he began humming a happy tune.

After three hours of furious labor, Stuart's column filed across the makeshift structure. Then the Confederate rear guard under Fitzhugh Lee set fire to the bridge. As Lee rode off at about 2 p.m., he looked back and saw through the smoke a squad of Union cavalrymen pulling up on the far bank. Cooke's bluecoats had arrived 10 minutes too late.

Richmond was still 35 miles away. Stuart's men cut south, then swung northeastward on a path roughly paralleling the James River. After a night's sleep, the column reached Richmond on Sunday, June 15. In three days, the troopers had ridden nearly 100 miles, all the way around McClellan; Stuart had lost one man, Captain Latané, and one artillery limber, which had bogged down at the Chickahominy. His jubilant men rode into the city to the cheers of the populace.

The boost to Southern morale was enormous. But far more significant was the effect the raid had on General McClellan. All along McClellan had felt apprehensive about his supply line to White House Landing. Now Jeb Stuart had easily cut that line — if only temporarily — and confirmed its vulnerability. McClellan decided to move his supply base south of the Chickahominy, along with the two corps now on the north bank. On June 18, the first supplies left White House Landing for a new base on the James River. That same day, Franklin's VI Corps moved south; Porter's V Corps would remain on the

looked like a sentinel and every jagged tree bending over the road like a vidette."

In fact, the Federals were in pursuit, under the command of none other than Stuart's father-in-law, Brigadier General Philip St. George Cooke, a Virginian whose own nephew was on Stuart's staff. When Stuart left Talleysville, Cooke's Union column was just four miles back at Tunstall's Station.

Shortly after dawn on the 14th, Stuart's men reached the Chickahominy but found the rain-swollen river too deep to ford. Stuart led his column downstream, expecting the enemy to fall upon him at any time, as he wrote later, "armed with the fury of a tigress robbed of her whelps."

north bank for the time being to guard the transfer of matériel.

Stuart, meanwhile, had reported good news to Lee. The northern tip of Porter's line was not anchored on a natural obstacle; it was "up in the air" and vulnerable to a flanking movement. Lee could now proceed with his plan for an attack. The key to his offensive was Stonewall Jackson's 18,500-man army in the Shenandoah Valley. Lee wanted Jackson to march from the Valley and outflank the Federal right wing north of the Chickahominy. At the same time, Lee's three divisions, about 47,000 men commanded by Major Generals James Long-street, Ambrose Powell Hill and Daniel Harvey Hill, would attack from the west and sweep eastward along the north bank, threatening McClellan's supply line to White House Landing.

In anticipation of Stuart's news, Lee already had sent Jackson reinforcements—Whiting's division and a brigade of Georgians under Brigadier General Alexander Lawton. These troops would help Jackson fight his way out of the Valley if necessary.

On June 16, Jackson started his soldiers on the 120-mile march to Richmond, then rode on ahead for a council of war with Lee and his top generals.

General Fitz-John Porter, McClellan's subordinate and close personal friend, sits surrounded by his staff in August of 1862. The woman at far right, identified by Porter as a Mrs. Fairfax, was a former slave who served, in the general's words, as his "chief cook and bottle washer."

At Lee's headquarters a mile and a half east of Richmond, Jackson sipped milk, refusing stronger libation, and let Lee and the other division commanders do the talking.

The timing of Lee's offensive depended upon the speed of Jackson's infantry, his fabled "foot cavalry." He agreed to have them in position to attack early on the morning of June 26.

Lee did not know that his Federal adversary was also planning an attack — on a nearly identical schedule. McClellan's bridges were built, the roads were drying and he had reinforcements: Brigadier General George McCall's Pennsylvania Reserve division of 9,500 men, transferred from McDowell's army to Porter's V Corps, plus seven regiments pulled from the defenses of Washington and Baltimore.

The goal of McClellan's attack, tentatively scheduled for June 26, was modest: He wanted to move a mile or so westward toward Richmond and take Old Tavern, where the road north to New Bridge on the Chickahominy branched off from the Nine Mile Road. This would be his first real advance since the Battle of Seven Pines, or as the Federals called it, Fair Oaks. It would bring his siege guns a step closer to Richmond.

To cover his attack, McClellan attempted on Wednesday, June 25, to advance the position of Major General Samuel P. Heintzelman's III Corps west from Seven Pines along the Williamsburg Road. Shortly after 8 a.m., Major General Joseph Hooker's division, supported by an artillery bombardment, started forward through swampy, wooded terrain. Hooker's men made some progress against Major General Benjamin Huger's Confederate division, but after three hours of fighting General Heintzelman inexplic-

ably called them back. McClellan ordered a renewal of the attack. By late in the day, the Union picket line had gained perhaps half a mile — at a cost of 626 casualties for the North and 441 for the South.

This little battle, variously known as Oak Grove or King's Schoolhouse, put McClellan closer than ever to Richmond, which was now less than five miles away. Even so, the affair would be little remembered but for the fact that it marked the beginning of a new phase of the Peninsular Campaign: a week of almost continuous fighting that people afterward would refer to as the Seven Days.

Robert E. Lee had witnessed some of the fighting that afternoon, and he was worried. McClellan's little push forward, coming on the eve of Lee's planned offensive, suggested that the Federal commander might know something was afoot.

Lee was taking an enormous gamble in massing his forces north of the Chickahominy. South of the river, he was leaving fewer than 25,000 men under General John B. Magruder to defend the entire four-mile-wide front east of Richmond. Magruder, outnumbered by nearly 3 to 1, had been ordered to stage a boisterous show of force to intimidate McClellan. Magruder was to simulate preparations for an attack by firing shells and marching his troops to and fro — by raising dust and making noise. Much rode on the success of the demonstration; if McClellan mounted a full-scale attack against him, the Federals might easily smash through. If Lee lost his gamble, he might also lose Richmond.

That night McClellan did in fact know that something was afoot. Over the past few days he had received reports that Stonewall Jackson was marching down to fall upon his

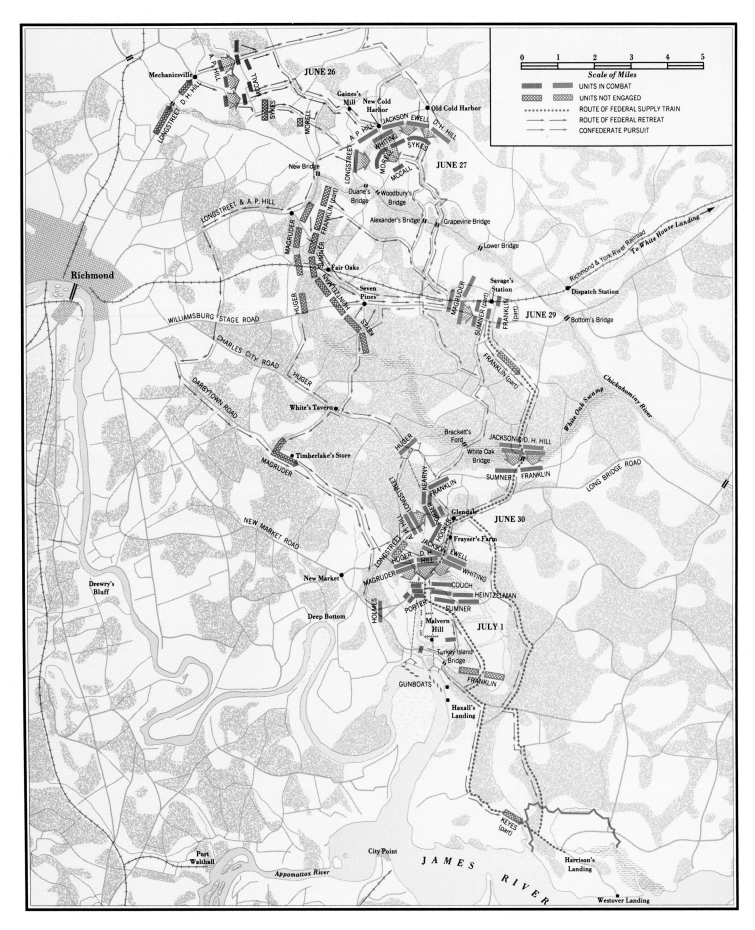

JUNE 26

Mechanicsville

A. P. HILL

MCCALL

D. H. HILL

LONGSTREET

SYKES

MORELL

Gaines's Mill

New Cold Harbor

Old Cold Harbor

LONGSTREET, A. P. HILL

JACKSON EWELL D. H. HILL

WHITING

MORELL

SYKES

MCCALL

JUNE 27

New Bridge

LONGSTREET & A. P. HILL

MAGRUDER

SUMNER FRANKLIN (part)

Duane's Bridge

Woodbury's Bridge

Alexander's Bridge

Grapevine Bridge

Lower Bridge

Richmond & York River Railroad

To White House Landing

Richmond

HUGER

Fair Oaks

Seven Pines

HEINTZELMAN

SYKES

MAGRUDER

SUMNER (part)

FRANKLIN (part)

Savage's Station

Dispatch Station

Bottom's Bridge

JUNE 29

WILLIAMSBURG STAGE ROAD

CHARLES CITY ROAD

HUGER

FRANKLIN (part)

White Oak Swamp

Chickahominy River

DARBYTOWN ROAD

White's Tavern

Brackett's Ford

JACKSON & D. H. HILL

White Oak Bridge

SUMNER FRANKLIN

LONG BRIDGE ROAD

MAGRUDER

Timberlake's Store

HUGER

KEARNY

FRANKLIN

NEW MARKET ROAD

LONGSTREET

A. P. HILL

PORTER

HOOKER

Glendale

Frayser's Farm

JUNE 30

JACKSON EWELL

Drewry's Bluff

HUGER

D. H. HILL

WHITING

New Market

MAGRUDER

COUCH

HEINTZELMAN

HOLMES

PORTER

SUMNER

Deep Bottom

Malvern Hill

JULY 1

Turkey Island Bridge

FRANKLIN

GUNBOATS

Haxall's Landing

Port Walthall

City Point

J A M E S   R I V E R

KEYES (part)

Harrison's Landing

Appomattox River

Westover Landing

Scale of Miles
0 1 2 3 4 5

UNITS IN COMBAT
UNITS NOT ENGAGED
ROUTE OF FEDERAL SUPPLY TRAIN
ROUTE OF FEDERAL RETREAT
CONFEDERATE PURSUIT

On June 26, Lee sparked the first major battle of the Seven Days by sending most of his forces north against Fitz-John Porter's V Corps on the Federal right near Mechanicsville. Porter fell back to the vicinity of Gaines's Mill, and on the evening of the 27th the advancing Confederates broke his lines, forcing him to retreat south across the Chickahominy. During the next three days, McClellan shifted his entire army south to the James. Lee's pursuing forces clashed with the Federals at Savage's Station and Frayser's Farm, and on July 1 both sides girded for a climactic battle at Malvern Hill.

Ambrose Powell Hill, a divisional commander in Lee's army during the Seven Days' Battles, attended West Point at the same time as George McClellan. According to legend, Hill bore a grudge against the Federal commander: Before the War, both men courted the same young woman, Ellen Marcy, but McClellan won her hand.

right wing from the rear. The ever-cautious McClellan grew even more so. He postponed the scheduled attack on Old Tavern and ordered Fitz-John Porter to send out a small force of cavalry and infantry to find Jackson and slow him down.

Early the next morning, Thursday, June 26, Lee stood on a bluff looking north across the Chickahominy toward Mechanicsville and waited for his offensive to begin. As the morning wore on with no sign of an attack against Magruder, Lee's fears about that front subsided. It was clear that Magruder's demonstration was intimidating McClellan's superior forces.

But Lee had a new worry — his own attack was not commencing. Three Confederate divisions had been on the south bank of the Chickahominy in position to attack since early morning: D. H. Hill's and Longstreet's in front of the two bridges leading directly into the little hamlet of Mechanicsville, A. P. Hill's less than two miles upstream in front of Meadow Bridge.

But the start of the attack depended upon Stonewall Jackson's three small divisions, which were supposed to attack the Federal right flank early that morning. A message sent by Jackson at 9 a.m. indicated that his vaunted foot cavalry was running six hours behind schedule.

Up at Meadow Bridge, A. P. Hill was even more impatient than Lee. Under the plan of attack, once he heard the sound of Jackson's guns he was supposed to advance through Mechanicsville and attack the Federal force dug in beyond Beaver Dam Creek. D. H. Hill and Longstreet were then to advance through Mechanicsville and join the assault.

At 36, Ambrose Powell Hill was the youngest of Lee's major generals, commander of the newest division and eager to prove his mettle. He was a bit of a dandy — a slender, handsome man, with long, reddish brown hair and beard, who liked to wear a flaming red battle shirt. He was also highstrung and cantankerous, traits explained in part by chronic ill health.

By 3 p.m., six hours had passed since Jackson sent his message, and Hill assumed that Jackson must surely now be approaching from the north. So, without notifying Lee, who was less than two miles downstream, Hill took his division across the river, swung right and began the offensive on his own. He drove back the Federal pickets, routed a regiment-sized outpost in Mechanicsville and deployed five brigades across the open plain beyond the town. Toward 5 p.m.,

fight at Mechanicsville between Beaver Creek —

Hill launched Brigadier General James J. Archer's brigade in the first in a series of piecemeal assaults on Porter's main defense line, entrenched on high ground behind Beaver Dam Creek.

Though Hill knew that the Federal front here was practically impregnable, he expected Jackson at any moment to outflank it. He even extended his left to make contact with Jackson so that together they could force the Federals to fall back.

At long last, shortly after 5 p.m., Jackson and his vanguard arrived at a place called Hundley's Corner, less than three miles from Hill's northernmost brigade. Jackson's march from the north had been extraordinarily slow. His columns had covered only 13 miles in more than 14 hours on the road — just seven miles since 9 a.m.

Certainly Jackson's men were tired; in the past 40 days the majority of them had fought five battles in the Valley and marched more than 400 miles. Their supplies were running behind, leaving them hungry and dispirited. To make matters worse, Union cavalry delayed the march by burning bridges, blocking the roads with fallen trees and harassing the troops from front and flank.

Jackson himself might have been laboring under some uncertainty. He did not know the boggy terrain north of Richmond, and his maps were inaccurate. He might not have fully understood Lee's orders, and might have been confused by Lee's failure to detail a staff officer to guide him into position.

The delay was explicable, but nothing could account for what happened when Jackson finally arrived at Hundley's Corner. He could hear the sounds of battle from the southwest — the boom of Federal artillery

Calls division and the rebels under Jackson

Emplaced on high ground commanding Beaver Dam Creek, Federal batteries under Brigadier General George A. McCall fire above the ranks of friendly infantry at Confederates massed in the line of trees along the creek.

and the crackle of A. P. Hill's musketry — and all he had to do to turn the enemy flank was push forward a mile or two. Instead, without so much as sending a message to Lee, he put his men into bivouac and bedded down for the night.

So astonishing was this performance that one Confederate officer later wrote that on this day Jackson "was not really Jackson. He was under a spell." The general was undoubtedly as exhausted as his men. During the past four days he had slept only 10 hours — and his associates knew him as a man who needed his sleep. "When he went to sleep he was the most difficult man to arouse I ever saw," wrote Dr. Hunter Maguire, Jackson's medical officer. And, said Maguire, "if his rest was broken for one night, he was almost certain to go to sleep upon his horse if riding the next day."

For whatever reason, Jackson went to bed early that evening while a near massacre was being enacted within earshot. The Federal position at Beaver Dam Creek was solid and unassailable. The defenders, George McCall's division of Pennsylvanians, were entrenched on a slope that rose from the east bank of the creek. Atop the crest were six batteries — 36 guns in all — that commanded the long open plain over which the Confederates were advancing from the west. The batteries rained a deadly accurate fire of shot and shell on A. P. Hill's troops as they charged across the flat land toward the creek.

Robert E. Lee, who had crossed over the Chickahominy at about 5 p.m. after seeing the smoke of battle, was little more than an anxious spectator at the hopeless assault. At one point, he tried to order Hill to break off the attack, but the message went awry. Seldom a man to show his emotions or assess blame—afterward, in his official report, he carefully avoided accusing Jackson of tardiness or A. P. Hill of a premature attack—he nonetheless reacted brusquely when Jefferson Davis and an entourage of Congressmen, Cabinet members and staff officers appeared unexpectedly at the edge of the battlefield.

"Mr. President," Lee said icily, "who is all this army and what is it doing here?"

"It is not my army, General," replied Davis.

"It is certainly not *my* army, Mr. President," retorted Lee, "and this is no place for it."

Lee was moving his other two divisions across the river and, toward sunset, he sent D. H. Hill's lead brigade to aid A. P. Hill's embattled troops. Brigadier General Roswell S. Ripley's four regiments came into action against the strongest Federal position of all, near Ellerson's Mill on the banks of Beaver Dam Creek. The caustic D. H. Hill later wrote, "The result was, as might have been foreseen, a bloody and disastrous repulse." One of Ripley's regiments, the 44th Georgia, lost 335 out of 514 men sent into action.

At about 9 p.m., darkness ended the fighting in the Battle of Mechanicsville, the second of the Seven Days' Battles. Lee, in his first major encounter, had failed miserably. He had applied less than one fourth of the available force; he had fallen far short of his first-day's objective—a four-mile advance to New Bridge to establish a link with Magruder on the south bank of the Chickahominy; he had lost 1,484 men killed and wounded. Confederate casualties lay along Beaver Dam Creek, a Federal officer observed, "like flies in a bowl of sugar." One Federal colonel reported that "the cries

of their wounded were heard plainly all through the night."

The Federals had suffered only 361 casualties, scarcely more than had the 44th Georgia Regiment alone. General McClellan, who had arrived at Porter's headquarters during the battle, was ecstatic. "Victory of today complete and against great odds," he wired Washington that night. "I almost begin to think we are invincible." He cabled his wife, "We have again whipped the Secesh. Stonewall Jackson is the victim this time."

For all his bravado, McClellan knew his right flank would be vulnerable when Jackson roused himself at dawn. During the night, McClellan ordered Porter to withdraw eastward to a second line of defense. By dawn, only a rear guard remained at Beaver Dam Creek to slow Lee's advance; the rest of Porter's corps was marching four miles east to another sluggish little stream, called Boatswain's Creek, which afforded an even more formidable defensive position. Marsh and fringes of pine trees bordered its steep banks. On the east bank, the ground rose to form a crescent-shaped plateau.

Fitz-John Porter deployed his entire V Corps on this high ground. Brigadier General George W. Morell's division held the left half of the line, and Brigadier General George Sykes's division of Regular U.S. Army troops the right. McCall's division, in the thick of the battle the day before at Mechanicsville, was held in reserve. Nearly 80 pieces of artillery were deployed along the crest of the ridge.

Porter's men hastily dug rifle pits and constructed crude breastworks with felled trees and pillaged fence rails. Then around noon, they settled back to wait.

When Lee discovered the Federal withdrawal early that morning, he sent his four commands eastward in three roughly parallel columns with the aim of hitting Porter front and flank. To the north, Jackson and D. H. Hill would head for Old Cold Harbor, hoping again to get behind Porter's right flank. Longstreet would drive along the north bank of the Chickahominy in support of A. P. Hill, who, in the center, would pursue Porter's rear guard.

A. P. Hill's lead brigade consisted of five regiments of South Carolinians led by Brigadier General Maxcy Gregg, a wealthy 47-year-old South Carolina planter. Gregg's men encountered the Federal rear guard around noon near a five-story gristmill called Gaines's Mill — the name applied to the battle that day. After a sharp skirmish, the Federals fell back.

A. P. Hill pushed on for a little less than a mile before reaching the crossroads at New Cold Harbor. There he found two narrow roads, one leading southeast and the other due south. Both these roads, Hill soon discovered as he sent his skirmishers forward, led for about 600 yards through open fields and fringes of pine trees down a slope to Boatswain's Creek — and both ran right into Fitz-John Porter's new defense line.

The resemblance to the previous day's situation at Beaver Dam Creek was uncanny: Again the Confederates were occupying generally open ground exposed to the fire of an enemy entrenched on the slope of a ravine. Today, however, Lee, who was with A. P. Hill, knew that Longstreet would be coming up soon on his right, and that D. H. Hill and Jackson were expected momentarily at Old Cold Harbor, just a mile to the left.

At 2:30 p.m., under the covering fire of his artillery, A. P. Hill started sending his six brigades forward against the center of the Federal line.

Gregg's South Carolinians were again in the lead, though they were somewhat the worse for wear. Exhausted from the previous day's assault at Beaver Dam Creek and from the skirmish at Gaines's Mill, some of the men had fallen asleep in a pine thicket with artillery shells falling around them.

But when the order to attack came, recalled a 14-year-old Confederate artillerist named J. D. Goolsby, Gregg's men awoke in a hurry. "What a shout went up," Goolsby wrote, "as these noble Carolinians, with their commander, passed through the battery in a double quick step." The young gunner watched Gregg's men surge toward the fire-spitting Federal cannon on the plateau; the field suddenly seemed to erupt into "one living sheet of flame."

The gale of Federal fire mounted savagely as Gregg's men, followed by the other brigades, advanced unevenly over a front about three quarters of a mile wide. By the time the Confederate lines reached Boatswain's Creek, all semblance of coordination between the brigades had ceased. With their view of flanking units blocked by timber and billowing smoke, the men struggled blindly through the swamp and tangle of brushwood on the edge of the creek.

Three regiments from Gregg's brigade somehow weathered the fire, crossed the creek and started clambering up the far slope. There they clashed head on with General Sykes's division. Sykes, a hard-bitten 39-year-old disciplinarian, had two regiments of volunteers in his division of Regular Army troops; one of these was the 5th New York Zouaves, flashy and fierce in their baggy red breeches and fezzes.

In this photograph from a broken glass negative, Federal engineers construct a plank road leading to a bridge across the Chickahominy River. They placed logs over a bed of stones and underbrush, then packed the gaps tight with dirt to form a hard, smooth surface.

The Zouaves, mounting what one Confederate called "the most desperate charge I ever witnessed," hit Gregg's 1st South Carolina Rifles and drove them back, inflicting losses of 60 per cent. Other Confederates came up in force, formed at the edge of the woods on the Zouaves' right and opened fire. Nearly a third of the Zouaves were already wounded or dead, and this new Confederate onslaught threatened a breakthrough.

Just then, as the Zouave line began to waver, the bearer of the regimental colors, Sergeant John H. Berrian, strode forward 30 paces in front and planted the flagstaff firmly in the ground. He was quickly joined by the bearer of the U.S. flag, Sergeant Andrew B. Allison, a transplanted Englishman and veteran of the Crimean War.

Officers shouted for the pair to come back, but the other Zouaves took inspiration from the show of bravery. They let out a yell, recalled one Zouave, Private Alfred Davenport, "so demonic and horrid that men in peaceful times cannot imitate it." Then, without orders, they rushed the woods and at bayonet point drove the enemy back to the trees lining Boatswain's Creek.

But more Confederates pushed forward in the wake of Gregg's attack. Private M. T. Ledbetter of the 5th Alabama plunged ahead through the swamp and found himself within about 15 or 20 paces of the Federal line across the creek. "I looked back to see if the boys were coming," he later wrote. "Just then I was shot through my right hip."

Ledbetter raised himself up on his hands, "like a lizard on a fence rail," and found that he was the only live Confederate in sight. His regiment had retreated.

Dragging his useless right leg, Ledbetter began his own retreat, crawling and hopping

39

under the galling fire of cannon and musket. A Minié ball severed his left thumb and tore into the wrist. Then, seeking cover in a deep gully, he looked back to see if Federals were in pursuit, and "just at that moment a ball drew a little blood from under my chin."

Ledbetter, thrice wounded, was sustained in his resolve to escape by a terrible fear —

"of being captured and lying in a Northern prison, in my condition." His route to the rear was so thickly strewn with Confederate dead and wounded that he had difficulty hobbling through. At last, more than 600 yards from where he was first hit, Ledbetter found shelter under a large oak tree. With the shells still bursting around him, he lay

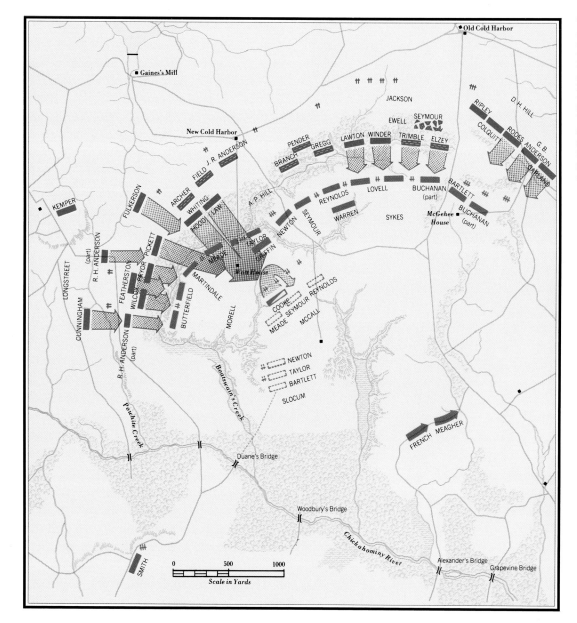

The Battle of Gaines's Mill began in earnest around 2 p.m. on June 27, when Confederate forces under A. P. Hill attacked Fitz-John Porter's V Corps behind Boatswain's Creek. Later James Longstreet came up on Hill's right, Stonewall Jackson arrived on the left, and around 7 p.m. the Confederates attacked all along the line. W.H.C. Whiting's division, led by John Bell Hood's brigade, pierced the Federal center, forcing Porter to withdraw across the Chickahominy River after nightfall.

there for an hour until litter-bearers found him and took him to a Confederate hospital.

A little after 4 p.m., A. P. Hill concluded that his "brave men had done all that any soldiers could do." They had been fighting for more than an hour and a half without reinforcement. He ordered his brigade commanders to break off contact where possible and rest their men until help arrived.

Longstreet had come up on Hill's right, but Lee wanted to delay his attack until Jackson got into position on the far left. However, Jackson was late again. He had taken a wrong road that morning and did not arrive at Old Cold Harbor until after 2 p.m., with three divisions and a large brigade trailing somewhere behind. D. H. Hill's division, under temporary command of Jackson that day, had preceded him to Old Cold Harbor.

Neither Jackson nor D. H. Hill was in communication with Lee, and it was about 4:30 p.m. before Jackson finally committed Hill's division on the far left of the Confederate offensive. Hill then advanced against his old West Point roommate, George Sykes. He drove straight south along the east side of the road from Old Cold Harbor and crossed the swampy headwaters of Boatswain's Creek.

Several of his regiments fought their way up through the tangled underbrush south of the swamp onto cleared ground. Here, an open plain 400 yards wide separated them from the Federal line. The plain was being peppered by three batteries of Regular U.S. artillery emplaced near a building called the McGehee House. Hill ordered his men to cross the clearing and seize the deadly guns.

One Federal infantryman found the battle discipline of the attacking Confederates nothing less than breathtaking. "We witnessed as complete a move by the enemy as could be made on drill or parade. They came out of the woods at double-quick, with guns at right-shoulder shift, and by a move known as 'on the right by file into line' formed the line of battle complete. We had not long to admire them. Forward they came, intending to strike our line on the right. Not a gun did they fire until within less than 50 yards, when after a volley they gave a yell, and charged, five lines deep."

The 20th North Carolina pushed back the Federal infantry supporting two pieces of artillery, then the Confederates waded into the artillerymen, who stood by their guns and bravely but futilely fought bayonets with rammer staffs, muskets with pistols.

No sooner had the Confederates seized the guns, however, than they themselves became the target of a heroic charge, spearheaded by the 16th New York, the vanguard of a division of reinforcements from the VI Corps under Brigadier General Henry W. Slocum. These men stood out in the straw hats they were wearing that day — bright yellow ones that the wife of their colonel, Joseph Howland, had recently sent down from New York. The men were the envy of the other Federals, who were wearing sweaty forage caps in the intense Virginia heat.

Howland's men swarmed forward and, in fierce hand-to-hand fighting, drove off the North Carolinians and regained the guns. By the end of the day, no one envied the 16th its bright hats, which had made inviting targets for the enemy; the battle cost the regiment 201 men, including Colonel Howland, who was severely wounded.

Meanwhile, in the Confederate center, A. P. Hill's battered division had finally received some help. One of Stonewall Jackson's trailing divisions, consisting of three brigades of hardened Valley veterans under Major General Richard Ewell, arrived on the field at about 4:30 p.m. and was sent by Lee to support Hill's left.

In the lead, Ewell's 15th Alabama had to cross a little swampy stream; one soldier, Private W. A. McClendon, sank up to his knee in the mud, losing his shoe. By the time he had retrieved the shoe and caught up with the advance, McClendon's company was under musket fire from Sykes's red-legged Zouaves. McClendon "sent a ball and three buckshot among them" and then looked over and saw his comrade, Tom Burk, go down. "A minie ball had hit him in the pit of the stomach," recalled McClendon, "and with each pulsation his life's blood would gush from the hole. In his delirium he made an unsuccessful attempt to stop the hole with his canteen stopper."

McClendon left his dying comrade and crossed the ravine. The Federal front was now about 50 yards away, and the noise of the battle was so deafening that McClendon said afterward he could tell when he had fired his musket only by the kick of the breech against his shoulder. He and the other Alabamians flopped to the ground and held on, but they could not dent the triple-tiered Federal line.

Two of Ewell's brigade commanders were early casualties. Brigadier General Arnold Elzey took a terrible wound in the face, and as he was being carried away all of his staff officers were cut down around him. Colonel Isaac G. Seymour was shot dead as he led the Louisiana Brigade forward, and soon thereafter Major Roberdeau Wheat, the colorful six-foot-four-inch, 250-pound commander of the battalion known as the Louisiana Tigers, fell riddled with bullets within 20 paces

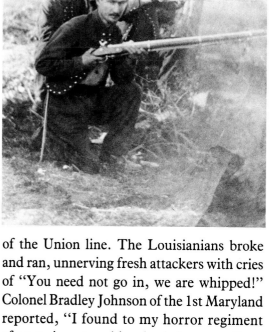

Zouaves of the 95th Pennsylvania, seen here deployed in skirmish formation, fought stubbornly at the Battle of Gaines's Mill, losing 112 men killed or wounded.

of the Union line. The Louisianians broke and ran, unnerving fresh attackers with cries of "You need not go in, we are whipped!" Colonel Bradley Johnson of the 1st Maryland reported, "I found to my horror regiment after regiment rushing back in utter disorder. The 5th Alabama I tried in vain to rally with my sword and the rifles of my men."

But some of Ewell's men had gained a foothold. Like an incoming tide each wave of attackers lapped higher on the slope of the ridge, in the face of what one officer called "a perfect sheet of fire." Through it all General Ewell, bareheaded, sword in hand, raged up and down his line, bellowing orders, prodding his troops forward. When the brigade of Georgians led by Alexander Lawton staggered under the enemy volleys, Ewell pushed them back into line shouting "Hurrah for Georgia!"

The battle now extended all the way to the Confederate far right, where Longstreet's men were locked in combat with Morell's Federal division. Originally ordered by Lee to make a "diversion," Longstreet on his own initiative had "determined to change the feint into an attack," and sent four brigades charging forward. As in the case of Ewell's assault, the Federal line held firm.

It was now past 5 p.m., and Robert E. Lee was running out of time. He still had not been able to coordinate all his troops for a full-scale assault up and down the line. Presently, the principal reason for this failure, General Stonewall Jackson, came riding down the road from Old Cold Harbor.

Lee did not bother to ask what Jackson had been doing all this time. He simply said, "Ah, General. I am very glad to see you. I had hoped to be with you before."

Having delivered this gentle rebuke, Lee explained over the heavy rattle of musketry in the background that he was preparing an all-out assault and wanted to get the rest of Jackson's forces up into line.

"That fire is very heavy," Lee said. "Do you think your men can stand it?"

"They can stand anything," said Jackson. "They can stand that."

While Lee worked to get the rest of Jackson's units into line, Fitz-John Porter waited apprehensively at his headquarters, the Watt House, atop the plateau. At about 6 p.m. he noted a sudden and "ominous silence"—a sign of Lee's preparations across the way.

Porter had done a masterful job. He had handled his defenses, according to his opponent D. H. Hill, "with an ability unsurpassed on any field during the war." Porter's line was still unbroken, but it had been sore-

In the midst of desperate fighting at Boatswain's Creek, Colonel Bradley Johnson halts his Confederate 1st Maryland Infantry and drills the ranks under fire after they faltered during a charge. The men quickly recovered, hurled themselves at the Federal line, and drove it back.

In this dramatic depiction by artist William Trego, troopers of the 5th U.S. Cavalry spur their mounts forward in a desperate charge to save Federal batteries near Boatswain's Creek. The gallant try was futile: Confederate infantry drove the troopers back and seized the guns.

ly tried. Ammunition was running low, and many of the Federals had been firing so long that their musket barrels were fouled.

Worse, Porter had committed all his reserve forces, including Slocum's division of the VI Corps, and his lines were now desperately thin. Shortly before 5 o'clock in the afternoon, Porter had dispatched a message to McClellan's headquarters asking for more reinforcements. Although McClellan had more than 60,000 men at his disposal, he relinquished only two brigades. Magruder was putting up such a big show that McClellan's corps commanders reported they needed every available man south of the Chickahominy to meet an expected attack.

At 6:30 p.m., Porter noted that the silence along his battlefront had ended. Darkness was still at least two hours away, and the din of musketry had resumed; more than that, it was rising to a crescendo that one Confederate brigade commander would later call "the heaviest I have heard on any field."

At last, after more than five hours of battle, Lee had all his troops in line. Never in the War had the Confederates concentrated so many men on a single battlefront — 56,000 men against Porter's 35,000.

The general assault began at about 7 p.m., though not all units advanced simultaneously. Among the last to march into action was Whiting's division, with brigades under Brigadier General John Bell Hood and Colonel Evander M. Law. When Lee saw Hood ride past, he singled him out for a quick briefing.

Hood was 31, a six-foot-two-inch giant with fair hair and beard. Born in Kentucky, he commanded the Texas Brigade — so called even though two of its regiments were from South Carolina and Georgia. Lee ex-plained to him that Porter's defenses had to be broken before dark.

"Can you break his line?" Lee asked.

Hood said he would try. Lee raised his hat and said, "May God be with you."

As Hood moved his brigade forward through the gathering twilight, he noticed a gap in the Confederate line. It was over to the right, beyond Law's brigade.

Hood quickly sent the 18th Georgia and 4th Texas swinging right, across the rear of Law and into the gap next to Longstreet's division. Hood ordered his men to hold their fire as they advanced. He dismounted and personally led his troops on, with the 4th Texas in the vanguard. They reached a slight crest where survivors of A. P. Hill's assault were still holding out, then passed through them and descended the long slope toward Boatswain's Creek into a hail of shells and musketry. Scores fell, but the others closed ranks and kept on — hunched over, someone observed, like Texans on a turkey hunt.

On the near bank of a ravine, about 150 yards from the Federal line, Hood paused to dress his lines. Here he gave the order to fix bayonets and charge at the double quick.

Hood's men surged across the swampy creek and up the slope, still without firing. They pushed onto the crest, just 10 yards from the Federal line. There, wrote one soldier, "the smoke was so thick that it was impossible to see twenty yards." And there, for the first time, they opened fire. At point-blank range, a wall of lead slammed into Brigadier General George W. Taylor's New Jersey Brigade. Lieutenant Camille Baquet, one of Taylor's staff officers, wrote: "The volley that fell upon the brigade was the most withering I ever saw delivered, for the men were totally unprepared for it. The

John Bell Hood, whose Texas Brigade spearheaded the Confederate breakthrough at Boatswain's Creek, was a superb combat leader. His rise from lieutenant to full general in four years was one of the most spectacular in the Confederate Army.

New Jersey Brigade broke all to pieces."

This was the breakthrough Lee had wanted. The Federal line began to crumble. Porter's left fell back — at first stubbornly and then in a state approaching panic.

In the confusion on the plateau where Hood had broken through, the greater part of two Federal regiments were cut off and captured. As the Confederates pursued the broken Federal ranks, they ran head on into artillery that had been massed behind Porter's left. Wheel to wheel the Federal batteries blazed away with double charges of canister. But there was no stopping the Confederates this time. As one artillerist recalled, "There was dreadful carnage in their ranks, but each horrible gap was instantly closed up, and the column pressed forward. When within twenty paces of the battery, at a

single round the whole front rank was carried away, yet still forward rushed the infuriated enemy to the very muzzles of the guns."

While the battery commanders struggled to get their cannon limbered up and off the field, General Philip St. George Cooke sent a squadron of his 5th U.S. Cavalry on a desperate attempt to save the guns. Bugles sounded the charge, and with sabers flashing the troopers galloped through their artillery and into the oncoming Confederates.

Lost in the smoke of the battle, one Texan heard the cavalry coming. He "felt the ground begin to tremble like an earthquake and heard a noise like the rumbling of distant thunder." Suddenly the horsemen burst through the smoke. But the charge was doomed. At 40 yards' range a Confederate volley sent horses and riders sprawling. Few troopers reached the Confederate line — those who did were killed. Private Pat J. Penn of the 4th Texas recalled that he "fired and emptied one saddle, and then lifted another man out of his saddle with the bayonet." Another cavalryman was carried off by his panicked horse with an enemy musket dangling from his body, the bayonet stuck to the hilt. Six of seven officers and 150 of 250 enlisted men who made the charge were killed or wounded. The demoralized survivors stampeded back through the Federal artillery. On their heels came the exultant Confederates, who captured 14 of 18 guns.

A complete rout of Porter's troops might have ensued but for the exhaustion of the Confederate attackers, the rapid descent of darkness and the arrival from the south of the two promised Union brigades.

As the beaten Federals retreated across the Chickahominy that night, the tired and overwrought McClellan expressed his bitter dis-

Hood's Texans move up to seize abandoned Federal guns behind Boatswain's Creek after the artillerists were driven off in fierce hand-to-hand fighting. So many of the artillery horses were killed or lamed that the Federals were unable to save their cannon.

appointment in an extraordinary fashion. In a telegram to Secretary of War Edwin Stanton, he reported the day's events, then leveled a stinging charge: "The Government has not sustained this army. If you do not do so now the game is lost." He concluded: "If I save this army now, I tell you plainly that I owe no thanks to you or to any other persons in Washington. You have done your best to sacrifice this army."

When this wire arrived in Washington, it so shocked the military supervisor of telegraphs that he censored the most offensive passages before handing the message to Stanton. The Secretary of War soon learned of its complete contents, however. Not only had McClellan further alienated President Lincoln, but he had infuriated the powerful and

vindictive Stanton. In time, the general's words would come back to haunt him.

While McClellan was trying to fix the blame on his own government, Robert E. Lee sent a message to his President thanking God for the Confederate triumph.

Lee's first victory was costly. In the Battle of Gaines's Mill, his army had inflicted 6,837 casualties, including 2,836 Federals taken prisoner. But the Confederates had lost 8,751 men, and among them were many brigade and regimental commanders whose absence would tell in the coming weeks.

Lee had, at the very least, silenced his critics. He had demonstrated that he was not wanting in audacity. Never again would anyone call him "Granny Lee" or suggest that he displayed any "tenderness of blood."

Flight to the James

"We were lavish of blood in those days, and it was thought to be a great thing to charge a battery of artillery or an earthwork lined with infantry."

MAJOR GENERAL D. H. HILL, C.S.A.

Late on the night of Friday, June 27, 1862, while Federal ambulances rumbled across the Chickahominy bridges with their burden of wounded and dying from the Battle of Gaines's Mill, George B. McClellan called a council of war. At 11 p.m., when his five corps commanders had gathered before a big bonfire in front of his headquarters tent, the general informed them of a monumental decision: The Army of the Potomac would abandon its entrenchments before Richmond and move south to a new position on the north bank of the James River.

The announcement astounded McClellan's officers. True, they were well aware that their chief had been shifting supplies southward for some time. In mid-June, alarmed by Jeb Stuart's spectacular ride around the Army of the Potomac, McClellan had sent transports to White House Landing to begin evacuating food and ammunition to a new depot at Harrison's Landing on the James. The commanders recognized as well that a complete transfer of supplies was now crucial. Once Fitz-John Porter's corps withdrew across the Chickahominy that night, there would be nothing to stop the Confederates from sweeping east along the north bank and severing the railroad supply line from White House Landing.

That much made sense, but what stunned many of those present at the council of war was the announcement that the entire army would also move south to the James, there to seek sanctuary under the protection of a flotilla of Federal gunboats and to await hoped-for reinforcements from Washington. McClellan was careful to label this movement of men and matériel a "change of base." But that was merely a euphemism for retreat, a point not lost on the men in the ranks.

When Generals Philip Kearny and Joseph Hooker, division commanders in Heintzelman's III Corps, got wind of the decision that night, they rushed to headquarters to protest. The fiery one-armed Kearny rebuked McClellan in such intemperate terms that one of his subordinates expressed astonishment that he was not sacked on the spot.

Instead of retreating, Kearny and Hooker wanted to attack Richmond. At this very moment, Federal pickets were less than four miles from the Confederate capital. With the arrival of Porter's corps, the entire army would be concentrated for the first time south of the Chickahominy. The army could shift its supply base to the James, Kearny and Hooker argued, and still operate against Richmond from its present entrenchments.

But McClellan was rattled. Magruder's noisy demonstrations south of the Chickahominy had only confirmed in McClellan's mind erroneous intelligence estimates that Robert E. Lee had at least 200,000 troops. The Federal commander believed that Lee's attacks north of the Chickahominy were only jabs preparatory to a knockout blow that would come south of the river. McClellan had to save his army, for he was convinced that only his army could save the Union.

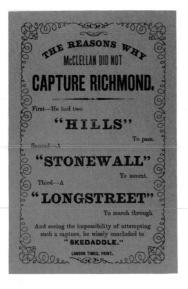

A pro-Southern broadside printed in England uses a play on names to credit four of Lee's commanders — D. H. Hill, A. P. Hill, Stonewall Jackson and James Longstreet — with halting McClellan's advance on Richmond. In fact, Stonewall Jackson made little contribution to the Confederate effort.

McClellan could have much more easily taken his army to safety whence it had come — back down the Peninsula toward Yorktown. But there would have been no way to avoid calling that a retreat. Moreover, establishing a base on the James, a score or so miles from the Confederate capital, left open the possibility of resuming the offensive against Richmond from the south.

Early on the morning of June 28, McClellan's army began withdrawing to the James. The long columns of men and animals, field guns and wagons streamed eastward on the Williamsburg Road, then south to the two bridges over White Oak Swamp.

According to McClellan's plan, two of his five corps would move on ahead to the north bank of the James to establish a defensive position on Malvern Hill. The three remaining corps would stay behind to slow the Confederate pursuit; then they would follow the retreat.

Though this great movement was taking place only a mile or two from Confederate pickets, it was carried out with such stealth that neither Lee nor his commanders realized what was happening. North of the Chickahominy, Lee awoke on June 28 to find the Yankees gone. Fully expecting McClellan to defend his supply line and his base at White House Landing, Lee assumed the Federals had retreated eastward along the Chickahominy's north bank. But when Lee sent Stuart's cavalry and a division of infantry east to seize the Richmond & York River Railroad, scarcely a Federal could be found. In fact, the Federals had destroyed their own railroad bridge over the Chickahominy.

Stuart cut the Federal telegraph wire along the railroad then raced on to White House Landing. The two-square-mile supply depot there, including lines of rail cars and five locomotives, already had been set afire by the Federals before they embarked on river transports.

By late afternoon, Lee was receiving reports of suspicious activity south of the Chickahominy. Loud explosions were heard as the Federal soldiers destroyed ammunition stores that they could not take with them; telltale clouds of dust swirled skyward from the forces retreating along the Williamsburg Road.

These signs, together with Stuart's report, suggested to Lee that McClellan was pulling out. Elated that the threat to Richmond had evaporated, Lee now wanted to catch and destroy McClellan's army. But which way was the enemy retreating — east down the Peninsula or south to the James?

Not until early the next morning, Sunday, June 29, did Lee get an answer. A reconnaissance confirmed that McClellan had abandoned his westernmost fortifications near Fair Oaks. And Ewell's troops, guarding Bottom's Bridge four miles to the east, reported no enemy activity. Since McClellan would most likely take this route if he were retreating down the Peninsula, the Federals were surely heading south.

Lee hastily mapped a strategy. His entire command was to take part in the pursuit. From their positions near Gaines's Mill, Longstreet and A. P. Hill would cross the Chickahominy at New Bridge and, in cooperation with Benjamin Huger, knife southeastward to intercept McClellan's forces below White Oak Swamp. Meanwhile, Magruder was to advance eastward against the Federal rear along the Richmond & York River Railroad. He would be aided by Jackson, who was to cross the Chickahominy at

Grapevine Bridge and link up with Magruder's left. If all went well, Lee would cut off and trap much of McClellan's army.

Since Lee did not expect A. P. Hill and Longstreet to intercept the retreating Federal column until the following day, the pressure this Sunday morning was squarely upon John Magruder. As he moved east with 11,000 men into the abandoned Federal entrenchments at Fair Oaks, the excitable Magruder was especially agitated. For four strenuous days, as his outnumbered troops mounted their demonstration, he had scarcely slept. He also suffered from indigestion and suspected that the medicine his surgeon had given him that morning was making it worse.

Reaching a point about three miles east of Fair Oaks, Magruder found much more to worry about. Here, drawn up in battle lines around the railroad depot called Savage's Station, were 40 guns and nearly half of McClellan's army: Samuel Heintzelman's III Corps, Edwin V. Sumner's II Corps and half of William Franklin's VI Corps.

Outnumbered nearly 3 to 1, Magruder pulled back and waited for help. His men were in position almost due south of the Grapevine Bridge, where Jackson was supposed to cross with 18,000 reinforcements. But Jackson was late again, for the third time in the past four days.

While Magruder waited, the Federals staged a spectacular display of fireworks in the area east of Savage's Station, setting aflame piles of supplies up to two stories tall. Shells and exploding barrels of whiskey rent the air as the soldiers destroyed what one envious Confederate officer called "all the apparatus of a vast and lavish host."

At about 5 p.m., Magruder brought up a siege gun mounted on an armored flatcar. This novel device had recently been worked out at Lee's behest to counter the expected threat of McClellan's big siege guns. The gun's rifled barrel, capable of hurling 32-pound shells, projected through a porthole in the car's protective shield of iron plate.

A locomotive pushed this rolling ironclad into range, and for the first time in the history of warfare, railroad artillery opened fire. But the debut was inauspicious. The gun's effect on the massed Federal batteries was minimal; Magruder saw no choice but to attack with his infantry just south of the railroad tracks. The Confederate assault made little headway. As usual, the Federal artillery fire was accurate and deadly; one shell mortally wounded Confederate Brigadier General Richard Griffith, a close friend of President Jefferson Davis.

Jackson never did show up; he sent word that he had "other important duty to perform" — presumably rebuilding the Grapevine Bridge, a task that took all day while Jackson overlooked a practicable ford not far away. Magruder, rattled, committed less than half of his force to the battle and brought up only one battery of artillery to supplement the railborne gun.

On the Federal side, matters were also confused. No one was formally in command. Without designating a field leader, McClellan had left Savage's Station early that morning to supervise the transfer of men and equipment south across White Oak Swamp. Heintzelman decided during the day that his corps was not needed at Savage's Station and marched his men off on the line of retreat without bothering to clear the move with anyone.

Nonetheless, the Federal lines held fast.

White House *(right)*, former residence of Martha Custis Washington and the plantation home of Robert E. Lee's son Rooney, was placed off limits to Federal troops by General McClellan. When the Army of the Potomac withdrew to the James River, McClellan ordered that the home be left intact, but on the 28th of June a vengeful soldier burned the historic structure to the ground *(below)*.

When the fighting ended at dark, old General Sumner, the senior officer present, was so elated at the repulse of the Rebels that he did not want to leave. "Why, if I had 20,000 more men," he declared, "I would crush this rebellion." Someone tactfully reminded him of McClellan's orders: Hold your ground until dark, then join the retreat.

Grudgingly, Sumner formed his men and, about 10 p.m., marched them south past the Union hospitals clustered near the station. About 2,500 sick and wounded soldiers lay there in houses, barns and tents — "a ghastly multitude," wrote Federal Chaplain James J. Marks, "bleeding, groaning, and dying." Under McClellan's orders, anyone who could not walk had to be left behind, along with enough surgeons, attendants and medical supplies to care for them. The ambulances drove south, empty and ready to receive fresh casualties from new battles.

The efforts of the Union rear guard at Savage's Station had been just what McClellan wanted. By 10 a.m. on Monday, June 30, all the Federal forces were safely across White Oak Swamp.

But McClellan's army was not yet out of danger. It stretched over the muddy terrain like an enormous snake, uncoiling for a distance of nearly 10 miles, its tail at White Oak Swamp and its head resting on the heights at Malvern Hill overlooking the James.

McClellan knew he had to protect the line of retreat for one more day to enable his supply trains to reach the sanctuary offered by the Federal gunboats on the James. Erasmus D. Keyes's IV Corps and Fitz-John Porter's V Corps had reached Malvern Hill, leaving McClellan seven divisions along the route of retreat. He posted two divisions under Franklin at White Oak Swamp. The other five divisions were deployed three miles south of the swamp on either side of the crossroads called Glendale.

Glendale, halfway between White Oak Swamp and Malvern Hill, was vulnerable to an attack by road from the west. It was also a dangerous bottleneck for the Federals. Here, near a farm owned by the Frayser family, the two routes of retreat from White Oak Swamp funneled into a single route, the Willis Church Road, which led to the James.

Lee's army was also in motion. It was a critical day for the Confederate commander — "the opportunity of his life," as E. Porter Alexander later described it. Lee's strategy was sound, but it would require better coordination among his subordinates than Lee had been able to achieve thus far.

It was a good sign for Lee that Jackson seemed to have shaken off the lethargy that had gripped him in recent days. The hero of the Valley Campaign crossed the Chickahominy before dawn on the rebuilt Grapevine Bridge and met with Lee at Savage's Station. Robert Stiles, a young artillery officer who witnessed the meeting, saw Jackson vigorously trace a battle diagram in the dirt with the toe of his right boot. Then Jackson stamped his foot and, in an apparent reference to McClellan, said, "We've got him."

Still, Jackson's progress south to White Oak Swamp was slow that morning. He took the time to round up about a thousand Federal stragglers who emerged from the thickets along the way. It was nearly noon when Jackson reached the ruins of the White Oak Bridge, which the Federals had burned less than two hours before. In the distance, about half a mile across the swamp, he could catch a glimpse of the Union rear guard: the last of the wagons, several batteries of artillery and

Spewing flames and artillery shells, an ammunition train set ablaze by Federal soldiers to prevent its capture plunges backward off a burning bridge into the Chickahominy River. A Federal chaplain who watched the train go by noted: "Bomb after bomb sprang from the fiery mass, hissing and screaming like fiends in agony."

ranks of infantry sprawled on a hill resting.

Now Jackson set to work like the Stonewall of old. He deployed 28 guns in a tree-shielded clearing to the right of the road. Shortly before 2 p.m., these guns leveled a fierce cannonade at the opposite hill; one Federal officer called it "a perfect shower of missiles." Then, with the skirmishers of D. H. Hill's division and a regiment of cavalry, Jackson forded the swampy creek for a personal reconnaissance.

The Federal rear guard consisted of two divisions under Brigadier Generals Israel B. Richardson and William F. Smith, and four batteries of artillery. These guns opened fire, forcing Jackson to hightail it back across the creek, followed by his cavalry. Hill's skirmishers, however, held on.

Jackson's situation was a difficult one; the Federal fire was so hot that it repeatedly drove away the soldiers he sent forward to rebuild the bridge. Yet the general brought no energy to bear on finding an alternative route for his troops.

After his initial burst of vigor that morning, Jackson lapsed back into the strange lethargy that had afflicted him since his arrival on the Peninsula four days before. According to the Reverend Major Robert Lewis Dabney, Jackson's chief of staff, physical and mental fatigue "had sunk the elasticity of his will and the quickness of his invention for the nonce below their wonted tension."

At around 3 p.m., while the opposing artillery boomed back and forth, Jackson lay down under a tree and went to sleep. He

Left behind after the Battle of Gaines's Mill, Federal wounded await the enemy's arrival in the yard of a home serving as a field hospital at Savage's Station. The men wearing straw hats belong to the 16th New York.

awoke an hour later and found time to write a letter telling his wife how much to give to the church — $50 — but he paid little attention to the problem at hand.

He made no attempt to scout for fords and disregarded promising information. A cavalry officer reported finding a cow-crossing suitable for fording 400 yards upstream; one of his brigadiers even came to him with the news that he had constructed a crude pole bridge a mile downstream and beyond the Federal right flank. Jackson ignored both of these reports. He simply sat there on a pine log as if attacking the Union rear guard were a project utterly beyond his capability. This curious lassitude was a mystery to all — and would remain so.

Jackson was not the only Confederate general who got bogged down that afternoon. A couple of miles to the southwest, another of Lee's columns — 9,000 men under Benjamin Huger — was also stymied.

Huger's division was one of the two Confederate columns aimed at the Glendale crossroads, where McClellan's cumbersome wagon trains were funneling south into the Willis Church Road. Huger was slanting southeast on the Charles City Road while, less than two miles to his right, the larger column of Longstreet and A. P. Hill — with Magruder scheduled to follow in reserve — was proceeding down a parallel route, the Darbytown Road. When Huger came into position in front of Glendale, the sound of his artillery was to be the signal for both columns to attack.

Before noon, when Huger's lead brigade was only two miles northwest of Glendale, it ran into an obstruction of felled trees left there by the Federals. Commanding the lead brigade that day was Brigadier General Wil-liam Mahone, a brave man but a quirky one, a hypochondriac who had his own private milk cow tethered to his headquarters wagon. When Mahone saw the trees blocking the Charles City Road, he made a snap decision. Instead of instructing his men to move the logs out of the way — they doubtless formed an imposing tangle — Mahone decided to bypass the obstruction. He ordered his men to hack a new pathway through the thick woods that bordered the road.

Up ahead, the Federal soldiers of Henry Slocum's division immediately saw what the Confederates were up to and redoubled their own efforts with the ax. While Mahone's Confederates worked away at cutting a swath through the woods, Slocum's men felled more trees to extend their obstructions.

Huger apparently saw nothing strange in this bizarre battle of the axes, noting in his official report only that "for such work we were deficient in tools." A 56-year-old former Regular Army staff officer, Huger had yet to show any flair for field command. A month earlier he had been blamed for his division's inactivity on this same Charles City Road during the Battle of Seven Pines.

By 2 p.m. Huger's soldiers had managed to win the battle of the axes, carving a mile-long path and emerging onto the road beyond the obstructions. But when he rode forward Huger saw a new obstacle: Deployed across the road on a rise, about a mile short of Glendale, was Slocum's division.

Huger moved a battery of artillery into position and, at 2:30 p.m., opened fire. Federal guns barked back. Huger's men took a few casualties, then withdrew to the cover of the woods. Though Huger outnumbered the Federals facing him by 3 to 2, he made no attempt to attack with his infantry. Like

Stonewall Jackson up at White Oak Swamp, Huger was finished for the day.

Not far to the south, Robert E. Lee, now with the column of Longstreet and A. P. Hill, was also only a little more than a mile from the Glendale crossroads. With 18,000 men, Lee had swung left from the Darbytown Road onto Long Bridge Road, and was approaching Glendale from the southwest. He was ready to attack the troops defending the crossroads as soon as he heard Huger's guns signal the beginning of the assault.

When Huger's brief cannonade was heard at 2:30 p.m., Longstreet ordered his own batteries to fire in acknowledgment. The Confederate exchange triggered action from Federal batteries on Long Bridge Road. Longstreet and Lee were then to the rear, where they had been joined by President Davis. The three, wrote Longstreet, were engaged "in pleasant conversation, anticipating fruitful results from the fight," when suddenly a Federal shell "burst in the midst of us, killing two or three horses and wounding one or two men. Our little party speedily retired to safer quarters."

Longstreet sent forward a brigade to silence the Federal batteries, and a brisk skirmish began on the Confederate right. Lee, however, decided to delay a general assault, having heard nothing from Huger or anything more from his guns.

Meanwhile, a fourth column of troops was converging on McClellan's line of retreat about three miles farther to the south. This column consisted of 6,000 troops under Major General Theophilus H. Holmes, who had brought his men across the James River on pontoon bridges at Drewry's Bluff.

Lee was not counting on Holmes for any hard fighting. His troops were too green.

Retreating from Savage's Station, the Army of the Potomac fords Bear Creek near White Oak Swamp. In the foreground stragglers doze and brew coffee, ignoring two mounted officers ordering them to their feet.

Moreover, Holmes was quite hard of hearing and at 57 was considered something of a has-been. He had been relegated to a backwater command south of Richmond.

Still, Lee hoped that Holmes could get within artillery range of the head of McClellan's column and do some damage. Such an opportunity arose at about 4 p.m. when Holmes received word that the Federal wagon trains were streaming up Malvern Hill on the Willis Church Road. Malvern Hill was less than three miles east of Holmes's position on the River Road, and he quickly started forward with six pieces of artillery. On the way, he met Lee, who had received a similar report and ridden south to see for himself. Lee suggested that Holmes bring his infantry up in support of the guns, then headed back north to Longstreet's position.

As Holmes's infantrymen hurried forward on the dirt road, their shuffling feet raised clouds of dust. This sign was clearly visible to the Federals on Malvern Hill, where Fitz-John Porter had posted his V Corps and part of the army's Artillery Reserve.

A few minutes later, at 4:30 p.m., when Holmes had his half-dozen guns in position about 800 yards from the train of wagons on Malvern Hill, havoc suddenly descended on the Confederates. Case shot and shell from no fewer than 30 Federal guns poured down. Even more terrifying were the salvos from several Federal gunboats anchored in the James River a half mile south of Holmes's column. A signal officer atop a brick farmhouse on the southern edge of Malvern Hill directed the fire of the gunboats. The shells were 100-pounders — so awesome that Confederates listening to the heavy black objects whoosh down called them "lampposts."

Some of Holmes's raw troops panicked.

Holmes himself had stepped inside a house by the roadside just before the first salvo; when he came out, he was the calm center of chaos — if only by virtue of his extreme deafness. He cupped his right ear and remarked, "I thought I heard firing."

Holmes pulled back his infantry and his decimated artillery. Lee's four-pronged assault had now been reduced to the single column under Longstreet and A. P. Hill on Long Bridge Road.

This critical day was slipping away and so,

Brigadier General Edwin Sumner, 65-year-old leader of the U.S. Army's II Corps, was the oldest active corps commander in the Civil War. Dubbed "Bull Head" after a musket ball glanced off his skull in the Mexican War, he was wounded twice during the Peninsular Campaign. McClellan described him as "fearless."

Lee feared, were McClellan's wagon trains. Lee did not know it, but the wagons Holmes had tried to attack were, in fact, the tail end of the Federal supply train. There now remained on the line of retreat not vulnerable wagons but seven divisions of Federal infantry — the two at White Oak Swamp and the five guarding the Glendale crossroads.

At about 5 p.m., in the desperate hope that Huger on his left and Jackson up at the swamp would hear the commotion and join in, Lee at last ordered the general assault on Long Bridge Road. Longstreet went in first, the battle lines splashing across swampy ground and moving uphill toward Frayser's Farm and the crossroads.

The Federal flanks were solidly anchored by two divisions: Kearny on the right and Hooker on the left. But the brunt of the Confederate attack slammed into the center, held by George McCall's division of Pennsylvania Reserves. The division was understrength, numbering fewer than 6,000 men. Tested at Mechanicsville and Gaines's Mill, they had slept only a few hours in the past three days.

For a time, McCall's infantry and artillery staved off Longstreet's charge. But the Confederate pressure finally proved too relentless for one of the regiments: The men of the 4th Pennsylvania Reserves broke and ran up the hill toward their artillery.

On the crest of the hill stood six Napoleon cannon commanded by Lieutenant Alanson M. Randol, a young West Pointer. Randol was reluctant to open fire lest he hit the Pennsylvanians as they came streaming up the hill. He later wrote: "On they came, the foe close behind them, till when within 30 yards I gave the command to fire; but it was too late. They rushed through the battery followed by nearly fifty of the enemy."

The 11th Alabama took the Federal guns in vicious hand-to-hand fighting. "Bayonets were crossed and locked in the struggle," reported General McCall. "I saw skulls crushed by the heavy blow of the butt of the musket, and the desperate thrusts and parries of a life and death encounter." One Alabama officer killed two Federals with his sword, only to be pinned to the ground by three enemy bayonets. Another Confederate officer took six bayonet wounds.

Now the 55th and 60th Virginia Regiments — A. P. Hill's troops — were sent charging at the Federal center to exploit Longstreet's breakthrough.

As he ran through Randol's wrecked battery, Private Robert A. Christian of the 60th Virginia came face to face with four Federal infantrymen. He managed to kill three of them with his bayonet, though wounded several times himself. The fourth man had knocked Christian down and was about to stab him when Christian's brother, Eli, came to the rescue and killed the attacker.

McCall's division collapsed in the face of Hill's charge. In the twilight, McCall was trying to rally his fragmented regiments when he blundered into the 47th Virginia. A volley dropped one of McCall's staff officers and scattered the rest; McCall then surrendered to the jubilant Virginians.

In the meantime, though, the other Federal generals had shown remarkable cooperation, despite McClellan's failure to appoint a field commander. Fresh troops from John Sedgwick's and Israel Richardson's divisions of II Corps were flung into action, Richardson's men marching south from White Oak Swamp when it became obvious that Jackson was not going to press his attack. Hooker held firmly on the left, and Kearny was able

After dueling with Stonewall Jackson's artillery at White Oak Swamp, the Vermont Brigade is ordered by Brigadier General William Smith (*on horseback, center*) to cover a gun crew (*right*) wheeling a fieldpiece to the rear. The scene was painted after the War by a brigade drummer boy named Julian Scott.

to halt Hill's breakthrough, then mount a counterattack that plugged the gap in the Federal line. The Confederates were driven back in savage fighting. Colonel Alexander Hays of the 63rd Pennsylvania reported, "It was muzzle to muzzle, and the powder actually burned the faces of the opposing men."

For a time it seemed that Kearny would regain all of the lost ground. But then A. P. Hill turned the tide with an inspiring display of bravery. Oblivious to the bullets flying around him, Hill rode to the front of the battle line, where one of Longstreet's regiments seemed ready to give way. Hill seized their flag and tried to lead them forward. When the men hesitated, Hill shouted, "Damn you, if you will not follow me, I'll die alone!" and then spurred his horse toward the Federal troops. Galvanized by the general's courage, the soldiers charged, repulsing Kearny's counterattack.

As night fell, the battle sputtered out in bloody stalemate. The ground around Frayser's Farm and the crossroads was covered with the dead and dying. General Hooker wrote, "The unbroken, mournful wail of human suffering was all that we heard from Glendale during that long, dismal night." In the battle that would be known as Glendale, or Frayser's Farm, Lee had gained a bit of shell-torn woods and a few Federal guns, but had lost more than 3,300 men. The Federals suffered 2,853 casualties, including 1,130 captured or missing.

Lee had also lost what he feared would be his last opportunity to cut off McClellan's retreat. The Federal wagons were safe at the James River, and the Federal infantry would be able to march south during the night to join the supply train at Malvern Hill.

Lee went to bed that night still not know-

ing why his strategy had failed, not understanding how 50,000 of his troops could have been within a three-mile radius of the battle on Long Bridge Road — indeed within hearing distance — and have failed to attack.

An epitaph for this day of lost chances already had been uttered unknowingly by Stonewall Jackson. Sitting down that evening to supper with his staff in front of White Oak Swamp, he dozed while still chewing his food, then jerked awake to announce: "Now, gentlemen, let us at once to bed, and see if tomorrow we cannot do something."

Early the next morning, Tuesday, July 1, Jackson's troops crossed White Oak Swamp unopposed and joined Lee at Glendale. Lee told his generals the pursuit would continue that day, south on the Willis Church Road with Jackson's force in the vanguard.

Lee once again kept bottled up whatever frustrations he felt at Jackson's curious inactivity during the previous afternoon. But Longstreet noticed that his chief looked "unwell and much fatigued." And a little later, when a newly arrived brigadier expressed his concern that McClellan might escape the pursuit, Lee let his feelings show. "Yes," he replied bitterly, "he will get away because I cannot have my orders carried out."

As he rode south on the Willis Church Road, Lee nonetheless hoped for one more chance to strike at McClellan. He suspected that his adversary would make a last stand at

Led by an officer waving his cap on his sword, men of the 55th and 60th Virginia overrun Battery E of the 1st U.S. Artillery at the climax of the battle at Glendale. The Confederate charge, according to a Federal general, was executed "without order, but in perfect recklessness."

Malvern Hill, three miles south of Glendale.

The hill was actually a large plateau, about a mile and a half long, three quarters of a mile wide and more than 100 feet high at the crest. It was separated from the James on the south by a strip of swampy ground and flanked east and west by creeks and ravines.

It was an ideal position to defend, as at least one Confederate general recognized. "If General McClellan is there in force," insisted D. H. Hill before Longstreet and Lee, "we had better let him alone."

Longstreet laughed and said, "Don't get scared, now that we have got him licked!"

Lee did not comment, apparently sharing Longstreet's belief that the Federals were demoralized and ripe for a licking.

McClellan's army was in fact on Malvern Hill — and in great force. Except for the wagon trains, which already had crossed the plateau and turned downriver toward Harrison's Landing, most of the Army of the Potomac was atop the hill, waiting for Lee.

William Harrison Rockwell, a 21-year-old private in the 18th North Carolina, was killed charging an enemy position near the Glendale crossroads. A Confederate officer recorded that the young man's regiment advanced shouting the battle cry "Stonewall!"

The Federal battle lines were arrayed in a rough semicircle on the northern rim of the plateau. The strongest concentration of men and guns guarded the left front, which was the most likely avenue of attack. Here, at the base of the hill, Willis Church Road emerged from thick woods and swamp and climbed a gradual slope through cultivated fields. Atop this slope, McClellan had three divisions of infantry and numerous batteries of artillery. Farther to the rear, around the century-old Malvern House, stood the bulk of the army's Artillery Reserve, nearly 100 guns practically wheel to wheel, including 14 mammoth siege cannon that had been laboriously hauled up the hill during the night. In all there were nearly 250 guns on the hill.

At midmorning on this hot, cloudless day, Jackson's column approached Malvern Hill to take up positions on the lower slopes. Immediately, the Federal artillery opened up, forcing Jackson's men to take cover in the woods on either side of the road. The Federal gunboat flotilla, standing by on the James just south of Malvern Hill, added to the awesome Federal firepower.

Shells were "smashing everything in reach," wrote a Confederate captain. "The Camden Rifles, a company of the 18th Mississippi, lay under a large oak tree. A ten-inch shell struck it about ten feet above the ground, cutting off the entire top. This fell on the Camden Rifles, killing several men and creating a worse panic than if ten times the number had been killed by bullets."

In the woods just west of the road, D. H. Hill sat calmly at a camp table on the exposed side of a big tree. When an officer urged him at least to put the tree between him and the Federal guns, Hill replied, "Don't worry about me; look after the men. I am not going

Battery C of the 3rd U.S. Artillery, commanded by Captain Horatio Gibson (*foreground, center*), stands ready to move into action. "Our superiority in artillery," wrote a Northern correspondent with McClellan's troops, "has saved the army from annihilation."

to be killed until my time comes." Suddenly, a shell exploded nearby, lifting Hill from his chair and hurling him to the ground. Hill shook the dirt from his uniform and resumed his seat — this time behind the tree.

By noon, Lee had most of his men moving into place in the woods and forming a mile-long crescent at the base of the plateau. W.H.C. Whiting was on the Confederate left with three brigades and D. H. Hill in the center astraddle the road with five brigades; two of Huger's brigades were on the right, where Magruder's six brigades were due to join them. In reserve were Ewell's division and Jackson's division on the left, and A. P. Hill and Longstreet on the right; Theophilus Holmes's small division was standing by a few miles to the west on the River Road.

In the previous battles, Lee had been plagued by the failure of subordinates to execute his careful plans. Now, however, Lee had no complex strategy — just the desperate wish to get in a final blow.

Presently, Longstreet returned from a reconnaissance to the right with an idea. West of the Willis Church Road, Longstreet had discovered a knoll that roughly matched in height the crest where Federal artillery was massed on the enemy left front, 1,200 yards away. He suggested that if 40 to 60 Confederate guns were placed on this knoll and perhaps 100 pieces deployed in a field in Whiting's sector half a mile east of the road, the Confederate artillery could effectively enfilade the Federal guns. Such a powerful cross fire, he reasoned, would be enough to create disorder among the Federal artillerymen and permit an infantry assault up the open front slope of Malvern Hill.

Lee gave the go-ahead. About 1:30 p.m., he issued orders to all of his commanders:

65

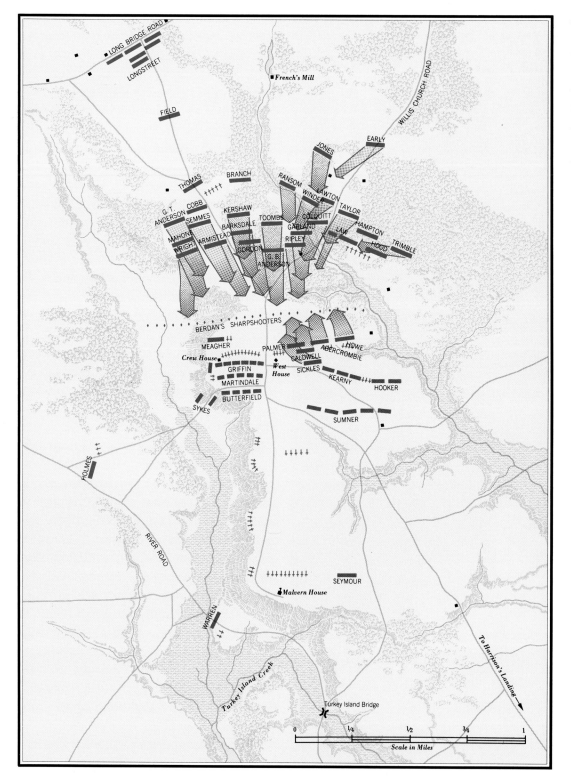

At Malvern Hill on July 1, Confederate artillery units went into action piecemeal and were soon silenced by counterfire from 250 Federal guns massed on the slopes and atop the hill. Lee then attacked with infantry divisions under Benjamin Huger, John Magruder and D. H. Hill, but each wave was decimated by the entrenched Federals and by fire from gunboats on the James. The Confederates were stymied; nevertheless, McClellan withdrew his army that night to Harrison's Landing.

Captain William Pegram, a shy, nearsighted student at the University of Virginia when the War broke out, was Lee's finest battery commander. At Malvern Hill, the day after his 21st birthday, he ran his guns forward to an exposed position and exchanged fire with superior Federal artillery until most of his men were killed or wounded and he was serving his last gun alone. He miraculously survived. In battle, said a fellow officer, Pegram was "supremely happy."

"Batteries have been established to rake the enemy's line. If it is broken, as is probable, Armistead, who can witness the effect of the fire, has been ordered to charge with a yell. Do the same."

This was a strange order to emanate from a tactician who prized precision in his directives. That Lee was entrusting the start of a general assault to Brigadier General Lewis Armistead just because he happened to be in a good position for observation was only part of the problem. In fact, the batteries referred to in the order had not yet been established — nor had Lee determined how they might be brought into position.

Lee did not even confer with Brigadier General William Pendleton, his chief of artillery. Pendleton had his artillery reserve of 90 guns somewhere in the rear on the troop-clogged road leading to Malvern Hill. He spent the morning looking for Lee and the afternoon searching in vain for suitable positions for his guns.

With the exception of D. H. Hill, who had sent his guns back to Seven Pines for refitting, the division commanders tried to bring up their own batteries. But they were frustrated by swamp and woods, and by accurate Federal shellfire. All during that afternoon, the Confederates managed to get into position scarcely more than 20 guns. Longstreet's scheme had called for at least 140.

Those pieces that did go into action were no match for the Federal artillery. As the Confederate batteries came forward one by one, they were knocked out or forced to withdraw. The most intrepid of the gallant Confederate gunners on the knoll across from Malvern Hill was Captain William Johnson Pegram of the Purcell Virginia Battery. A bespectacled, scholarly young man,

Pegram had been engaged in every battle of the past five days and already had lost more than half of his 80 men. By 3 p.m., only one of Pegram's six guns remained in action, and he was serving it himself.

Outgunned and outmanned though they were, Pegram and his compatriots in the artillery nonetheless managed to instill fear — and inflict casualties — among the Federal infantrymen waiting on Malvern Hill. A Federal sharpshooter, Charles A. Stevens, thought that troops seldom had "lain so long under as hot a fire as my fellows did. It is the most trying position a soldier has to endure, to stand these horrid missiles, crouched low, seeing them strike all about him, hearing them burst all around him, and yet unable to move or do a thing but wait in that awful suspense. Occasionally, yes frequently, some poor fellow picks up his leg or his arm, and hobbles off to the rear; then some fellow, less fortunate, had *to be* picked up."

At about 3 p.m., Lee realized that he would not be able to get enough guns into place to carry out Longstreet's plan. Without formally revoking his earlier order, he abandoned his idea of an infantry assault up the front slope. He rode over to the far left, hoping that he might find a place there to flank Malvern Hill and force the Federals to abandon their position.

Lee's search proved futile, but shortly after he returned from the reconnaissance, about 4 p.m., opportunity seemed to present itself and Lee pounced.

Hope came in the form of two messages that arrived almost simultaneously. One message was from Whiting on the left. Whiting had seen a movement of Federal troops on the hill and had misinterpreted it. Actually, General Sumner was merely shifting the lines of his II Corps, but Whiting believed that the Federals might be withdrawing from Malvern Hill and notified Lee to that effect.

The other message was from Magruder on the right. He reported that a formidable advance had been achieved there by Armistead who, under Lee's now-abandoned order, was to have signaled the general assault by charging with his brigade.

What had actually happened on the right was considerably less than Magruder's message implied. About an hour before, Armistead's men had become irked when Federal skirmishers, positioned in a field at the bottom of a steep bluff on the northwest corner of Malvern Hill, had started firing at them from behind shocks of newly harvested wheat. Without waiting for orders from Armistead, the Confederates sprang forward from the woods and dashed into the wheat field, driving the skirmishers back.

When Federal artillery began punishing Armistead's troops, they took refuge in a ravine at the near edge of the field, where they were joined by their commander. Armistead, though only recently promoted to brigadier, was a grizzled veteran of the Mexican War with a reputation as a bold fighter: He had been expelled from West Point, it was said, for breaking a plate over the head of fellow cadet Jubal Early.

Magruder arrived in the woods behind Armistead's advance position at about this time — hours late because his six brigades had taken the wrong road to Malvern Hill.

Magruder was not only late; he was exhausted, having marched and countermarched for 18 hours the previous day. He was ill and in such a state of excitement that many thought he was drunk. Someone handed Magruder the obsolete order for a general

assault. He read it, saw Armistead's brigade at the edge of the wheat field and leaped to a conclusion: He immediately notified Lee that Armistead had advanced.

Magruder's message, combined with Whiting's information that the Federals appeared to be pulling out, was too much for Lee to resist. Determined not to let McClellan get away this time, Lee sent verbal orders to Magruder telling him to advance immediately. "Press forward your whole line and follow up Armistead's success."

Magruder had been reproached by Lee on Sunday for lack of vigor in pursuing the Federals at Savage's Station; this time he would obey orders to the letter, even though neither his infantry nor his artillery were yet in position to attack. At 4:45 p.m. he ordered the assault, sending forward the troops readily at hand — two of Huger's brigades under William Mahone and Ambrose Wright.

Huger's troops emerged from the woods, about 2,500 men in all, yelling and cheering. Mahone was intent on redeeming himself after his so-called battle of the axes. Brigadier General Wright, a 36-year-old Georgia lawyer, was exuberant, bareheaded, waving his hat on the tip of his sword.

Their line of attack would carry them for nearly half a mile through wheat and meadow toward the bluff atop which Federal guns were clustered around the old Crew farmhouse. The landscape reminded one of Mahone's soldiers, George Bernard, of a nearby county where he had hunted as a boy. As Bernard marched to the attack, he wrote later, "a crowd of memories rushed upon me. I would have gladly then ended the war."

As the two brigades passed to the right of the ravine where Lewis Armistead's troops were still hugging the ground, the men

Firing over their own battle line Federal gunners on the slop of Malvern Hill blaze away Confederate infantry advanci across the open ground in th distance. Of the battle th culminated the Seven Day McClellan proclaimed: "I dou whether, in the annals of wa there was ever a more persiste and gallant attack, or a more co and effective resistance

jumped up shouting their welcome and joined the attack. The Confederates were now long lines of gray moving through the golden wheat into a storm of shot and shell.

George Bernard's regiment, the 12th Virginia, moved forward through the withering fire to a point about 150 yards from the Federal infantry, arrayed before their artillery. In the face of the Federal volleys the 12th fell back, then rallied and returned to the charge. But the Federal infantry line was "seemingly immovable," wrote Bernard. "It stood as if at a dress parade."

The cheers of the charging Confederates drifted back toward the center of the line near Willis Church Road, where D. H. Hill was lounging in the saddle smoking a cigar. Hill heard the yelling and recalled the terms of Lee's old assault order: "Armistead . . . has been ordered to charge with a yell. Do the same." Believing that this order was still in effect, Hill hurried his five bri-

gades to the attack sometime after 5 p.m.

From the edge of the woods where Hill launched his assault, it was about 800 yards to the Federal line. Unlike the terrain on the Confederate right, where the steep bluff provided Huger's men a modicum of protection from artillery fire in the hollows and ravines under its brow, the gradual incline before Hill's men offered no hope of cover.

Moving on a half-mile-wide front on either side of the road, Hill's troops marched directly into the mouths of the Federal cannon. As Colonel John B. Gordon advanced with

his brigade on the right of Hill's line, men began dropping all around him. A shell exploded nearby, killing half a dozen Confederates. The explosion tore the handle off Gordon's pistol, pierced his canteen and ripped away the front of his coat, leaving him shaken but otherwise unscathed.

The storm of Federal artillery fire was so intense that the 3rd Alabama of Gordon's brigade lost six color-bearers and suffered casualties amounting to more than half of the regiment. Even so, the men of the 3rd got to within 200 yards of the Federal defenses —

The U.S. Navy gunboats *Galena* *(left)* and *Mahaska* lob shells over Malvern Hill at Confederate positions beyond. Atop the farmhouse at center, a signal corpsman wigwags firing distance and direction to the gunships, while columns of Federal infantry wait in reserve on the near slope. The notations that appear on the sketch were made by the artist.

farther than any of Hill's other units. There, Gordon ordered his men to the ground, where they desperately tried to find cover behind the slightest undulation of earth, even the furrows left by a farmer's plow.

As the grayclads surged forward, the Federal gunners switched from shot and shell to case and canister for a lethal shotgun effect. The devastation was awful to behold. "Our batteries," said James Cooper Miller of the 2nd Delaware, "literally cut lanes through their ranks." Federals watched in horror as the onrushing waves of Confederates seemed to explode before their eyes. Knapsacks, hats, rifles, fragments of bodies flew through the air in grisly tableaux that witnesses would recall decades later. "It was not war," D. H. Hill wrote. "It was murder."

Colonel Henry J. Hunt, McClellan's 42-year-old chief of artillery, handled the guns superbly. Though three horses were shot from under him, he continued to shuttle new batteries to the front and keep the caissons of ammunition rolling forward. One battery expended no fewer than 1,392 rounds. In another, where ammunition ran low, the men claimed later to have cut the trace chains from their horse's harness and crammed the chains into the cannon, sending them whistling through the opposing ranks.

When the broken lines of Confederates came within musket range, the blueclad infantry took over. Facing D. H. Hill's charge at the Federal center, the men of the 105th Pennsylvania had each been provided with 150 rounds of ammunition and, wrote the unit's historian, "not a man left his post while he had a cartridge left." To their right, the 61st New York was firing so rapidly, wrote Sergeant Charles Fuller, that "the gun barrels became heated to the point that they could not be grasped and the men held their guns by the sling strap."

It was now about 6 p.m. In the center, D. H. Hill's brigades were breaking and falling back. On the right the remnants of Huger's three brigades huddled beneath the brow of the bluff, 75 yards from the Federal guns. To their right, Huger's last brigade, under Brigadier General Robert Ransom, stormed the bluff from due west of the Crew farmhouse and fought to within 20 yards of the enemy before retreating in the face of canister and musketry that Ransom reported as "beyond description."

Meanwhile, Magruder had finally begun bringing his own brigades into action, but they came up piecemeal and in confusion. When the 15th Virginia Regiment reached the meadow at the base of the hill, a shell fragment cut down its commander, Colonel Thomas P. August. The stretcher-bearers started to carry him away, but August, severely wounded in the leg, made them stop. "Boys," he shouted to his troops, "remember you belong to the old 15th Virginia, remember you are fighting for your homes and your firesides. Give them hell, damn 'em!"

Scarcely had August spoken, one witness recalled, when "the stretcher-bearers were struck down and the colonel, still bleeding, was tumbled ingloriously into a ditch."

Minutes later, August's replacement, Major John Stewart Walker, was preparing to lead the regiment up the hill when he too was hit; he died soon afterward in the arms of his brother, Captain Norman Walker.

The daylight was fading into a dusk hastened by the great pall of sulfurous smoke that belched from the Federal cannon.

Still, despite their losses, Magruder's fresh brigades came on. Groping forward through the haze, they stumbled across carpets of the dead and dying. More than half of the casualties littering meadow and wheat field were victims of the Federal artillery — "an unprecedented thing in warfare," noted D. H. Hill. Many of the bodies were horribly mutilated — limbless, headless torsos scarcely recognizable as men. So great was the confusion that one Confederate regiment, the 10th Louisiana, advanced over the prone but very much alive bodies of an entire regiment of compatriots who, obscured by dusk and smoke, appeared to be so many corpses.

Though the Federals held the upper hand, they had all they could handle from Magruder's men. Fitz-John Porter was worried that the Confederates might yet break through as they had, decisively, at Boatswain's Creek. He posted several batteries in positions where they could sweep the field with double canister, ordering them to stop any advance, even "at the risk of firing upon friends."

Then Porter called for reinforcements. Sumner and Heintzelman each sent a brigade, and Porter personally led one of them in a countercharge. Suddenly, a large Confederate force loomed out of the smoke and gloom only 50 yards away. Porter said later that the enemy "rose and opened with fearful volleys upon our advancing line. I turned to the brigade, which thus far had kept pace with my horse, and found it standing 'like a stonewall,' and returning a fire more destructive than it received and from which the enemy fled." Porter's horse was struck and threw him to the ground. Fearing that he might be captured, he destroyed his diary and dispatch book; but as it happened he managed to return safely to his lines.

Meanwhile, at the request of another worried Federal general, Samuel Heintzelman,

McClellan had put in a brief appearance on Malvern Hill to buck up the troops — one of his few battlefield appearances thus far in the Seven Days. Although his generals had been fighting without any overall field commander, the issue was never really in doubt. The Federals had nearly seven divisions of infantry in reserve. These reserves, while taking an occasional casualty from the sporadic Confederate artillery fire — and some from their own gunboats — had time enough to chase down stray pigs for supper and to simply sit and marvel at the incredible courage of their enemy. Many Federals were convinced, wrote one soldier, that the Rebels "had been rendered insensible to fear by whisky drugged with gunpowder."

The valor of the Confederates was extraordinary — and futile. Jackson was moving up his own troops and Ewell's divisions to reinforce D. H. Hill, but too late. Whiting remained idle on the Confederate left, and Lee did not call up Longstreet and A. P. Hill from reserve on the right or Holmes from the River Road. There would be no eleventh-hour rallying of Lee's line, no majestic general assault as at Gaines's Mill.

Toward 9 p.m. darkness came and the sound of musketry died away. Federal cannon boomed for another hour or so, the burning fuses of their shells describing fiery arcs through the inky dark. Then these guns, too, fell silent, to be replaced by the pathetic cries of Confederates who had fallen on the slopes of Malvern Hill. "One in particular," wrote a Federal lieutenant, "we could hear for hours in the same strained, high-pitched key, alternately praying and cursing." Confederate casualties had totaled 5,355.

That night the Army of the Potomac gathered up its own wounded — its losses were

Greeted by pillars of smoke rising from friendly campfires, the rear guard of the Army of the Potomac completes the eight-mile march from Malvern Hill to Harrison's Landing. While one Federal soldier admitted that he was unsure whether the army had made "an inglorious skedaddle or a brilliant retreat," Major General Joseph Hooker could scarcely conceal his disgust. "We retreated," he said, "like a parcel of sheep."

397 killed, 2,092 wounded and 725 missing — and followed the path of its supply wagons to Harrison's Landing. At dawn, cavalry Colonel William Averell, commanding the Federal rear guard atop Malvern Hill, peered down through the mist at the slopes and saw the horror he had been hearing all night. "Dead and wounded men were on the ground in every attitude of distress," he wrote. "A third of them were dead or dying, but enough were alive and moving to give to the field a singular crawling effect."

The Seven Days' Battles were over and, for now at least, Richmond was safe. President Davis issued an official proclamation of thanksgiving. Yet Southern gratitude for Lee's achievement was tempered by grief at the enormous cost. Overall, Lee had lost 20,614 men, nearly one fourth of those in his command when the Seven Days began. Of the casualties, all but 875 — those missing or captured — lay dead or wounded. The losses among Confederate officers were staggering. Ten brigade commanders and 66 regimental commanders were killed or wounded.

The Federal toll was considerably less — 15,849 in all, including the unusually large number of 6,053 missing and presumed captured. McClellan had saved most of his army — through a movement he termed "unparalleled in the annals of war." No words of McClellan's could disguise the fact that he had been driven to retreat, yet Lee himself was less than satisfied. In his official report, the Southern commander noted the failures of his subordinates and said: "Under ordinary circumstances, the Federal Army should have been destroyed."

Faces of an Army Forged by Fire

After the Army of the Potomac retreated to Harrison's Landing on the James River in July, it sat in the withering heat for the next six weeks awaiting new orders. During this respite, an enterprising photographer named Alexander Gardner visited the Federal camp to take portraits of the exhausted troops as they tended their wounds and reflected on a campaign gone awry.

Of 160,000 Federal soldiers sent to the Peninsula, less than 90,000 able-bodied men remained; the rest were either dead, wounded, captured, or laid low by disease. "This army left well equipped with everything a soldier needs," one private lamented. "Now, what a change. And who is responsible? The men feel that something is loose and can't find what it is."

Still, most of the soldiers retained their faith in General McClellan — for whom, said one, they would "fight to the last." And they took pride in knowing that they had fought the best Confederate troops on equal terms. But to these bloodied veterans, praise of their effort somehow rang false. As a private in the 5th New York Volunteers explained: "Eloquence and eulogy were swallowed up in the stern realities of the dead and dying, the sick and wounded left behind, the unknown and unremembered graves, and the individual suffering of every survivor."

Major General Samuel P. Heintzelman (*center*) and officers of his staff sit for a group picture by Alexander Gardner at their camp in the woods near Harrison's Landing. The photographer's glass negative was later damaged.

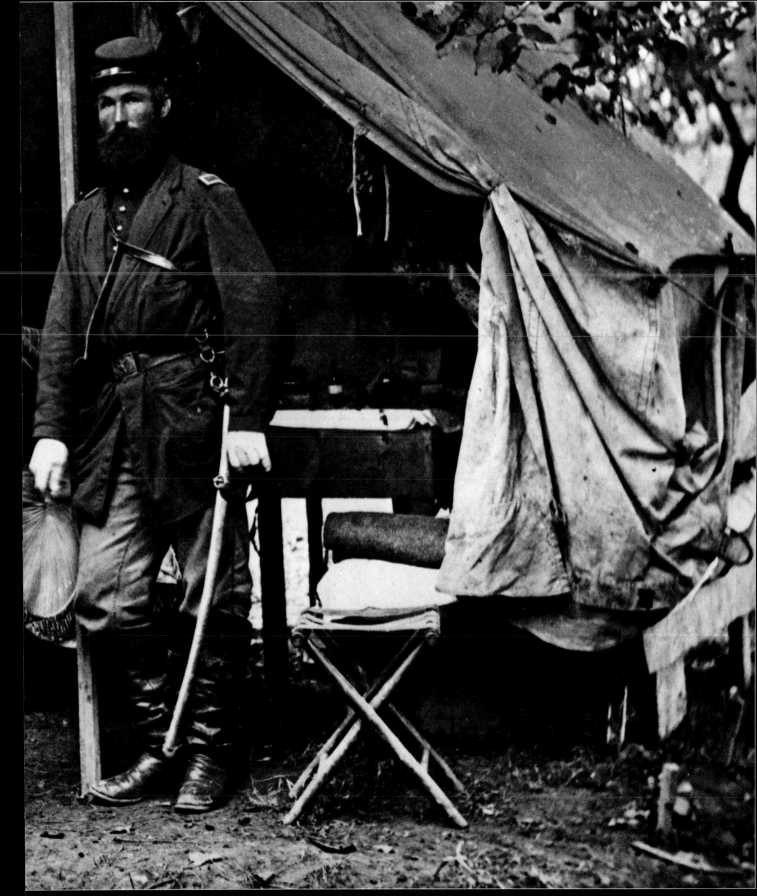

ringing laugh is seldom heard," a soldier wrote. "The men go dragging along with sad and care-worn faces."

Colonel James H. Childs of the 4th Pennsylvania Cavalry *(standing)* poses with his staff officers. Childs, described by one of his men as a "commanding presence, courteous and affable," was killed at the Battle of Antietam on September 17, 1862.

His tent flaps raised to let in the breeze, Lieutenant Colonel Samuel W. Owen dozes through a hot afternoon. The liquor bottle on Owen's cot was placed there by a mischievous onlooker.

Battle-hardened officers of the 3rd
Pennsylvania Cavalry gather before a
field tent for photographer Gardner.
Their troopers successfully covered
the Federal retreat from Malvern
Hill. Of the cavalrymen, General
McClellan wrote in late July 1862:
"Our men look like real veterans
now — tough, brown and fearless."

PRIVATE WILLIAM
MCILVAINE JR.

An Artist's View of the Peninsula

For George Alfred Townsend, a war correspondent, the swirling Federal retreat to Harrison's Landing was "marked by constantly increasing beauties of scenery." For men of the Army of the Potomac, who were fighting and dying daily in the steaming swamps and dense forests, plagued by mosquitoes, drenching rain and searing heat, nature's grandeur was the last thing on their minds.

Remarkably, one soldier did share Townsend's appreciation for the Peninsula's scenery. He was a 48-year-old private in the 5th New York Volunteers, or the Duryée Zouaves, named William McIlvaine Jr. *(self-portrait, above)*. A landscape artist by profession, McIlvaine was assigned to brigade headquarters behind the front lines. While the fighting raged — a third of the men in his regiment were killed or wounded at Gaines's Mill — McIlvaine painted the watercolors shown here, faithfully recording with his brush the setting, if not the carnage, of the terrible Seven Days.

Federal guards line the porch of White House, overlooking the Pamunkey River. On land nearby, General McClellan set up his headquarters and a vast supply depot.

Their arms stacked neatly in the shade, Federal soldiers near White House inspect St. Peter's Church, where George Washington was married. "Finding one-self alone within that historic building," General McClellan wrote, "it was a natural impulse to invoke the aid of God."

A barge laden with supplies and cannon moves slowly up the sluggish Pamunkey River, bound for a depot near White House Landing.

near New Kent c.H. May 13 1862

Zouaves of the 5th New York
Volunteers halt to rest along
a forest road near New Kent
Court House. Members
of the unit's famous color
guard — each man more than
six feet tall — display the
flag of the United States.

The day his regiment was decimated at Gaines's Mill, McIlvaine was five miles away, painting this view of the Federal camp at Savage's Station on the Richmond & York River Railroad. Two days later, the Federals burned the camp and retreated, leaving behind 2,500 sick and wounded.

After an exhausting day of marching and fighting, soldiers relax around a campfire in a thick wood near the Chickahominy River. Although the nights were warm, fires were welcome for the light and cheer they provided.

A column of Federals bypasses a stagnant stream on a corduroy road, made of logs laid side by side. Such boggy areas would have been impassable if the men had not corduroyed miles of old country lanes.

In the moonlight, a Zouave picket leans on his rifle — a relaxed stance violating regulations that a picket's weapon must never touch the ground.

Federal cavalry and artillery prepare to take up defensive positions atop Malvern Hill on June 30, 1862. In the distance Federal gunboats patrol the James River.

McIlvaine painted this scene of camp life while the Battle of Malvern Hill was raging just a few miles away. In the foreground, cooks busy themselves at a mess tent; farther off, cavalrymen water their horses in the James.

James River — near Camp of 5 — July 1862

After days of grueling marching, soldiers bathe in the James while others wash vermin-infested clothing. Many had lost their knapsacks and had only the clothes on their backs.

Taking the War North

"We are going through a sort of picking over and sifting process. A brigade put here and another countermarched to where it was a week ago. What they are going to do and when they are going to do it I don't know."

LIEUTENANT JAMES GILLETTE, 3RD MARYLAND INFANTRY, U.S.A.

In the aftermath of the Seven Days' Battles, the rival armies lay bloodied, exhausted and sweltering in the humid July heat. Operations dwindled to wary patrols, halfhearted feints and accidental skirmishes. The hardest fight was against malaria in the swampy lowlands dissected by the James River and its tributaries.

That July of 1862 was a time for rest, resupply and reorganization. And it was a time for painful reappraisal. What did the armies have to show for their heavy losses in the campaign just ended? Not nearly enough — that was the verdict both North and South.

The North was in a tumult. Gone was the grim resolve that had united contentious factions after the humiliating rout of the Federal army at Bull Run exactly a year before. The Union had split along party lines, with Republicans blaming Democrat McClellan for his army's failure to take Richmond, and Democrats accusing high Republicans of a conspiracy to oust their champion. To some observers, such partisan wrangling was itself partly responsible for the long casualty lists, which continued to grow for weeks as more and more men succumbed to wounds and disease. Said an embittered cavalry officer from Massachusetts: "We have been divided by our leaders, thrashed, aye thrashed, and now we are struggling for our existence."

In the South, the news that General Lee's army had warded off McClellan's mighty thrust was greeted with pride and relief. Nevertheless, Southerners noted with concern that all the bleeding and dying had not altered the basic situation in Virginia. Lee's army and Richmond were still in jeopardy, sandwiched between McClellan's army at Harrison's Landing to the south and three Federal corps to the north and west.

Critics called for an end to the passive strategy laid down by Jefferson Davis, who had been anxious to propitiate the European powers by showing that the Union was the aggressor. In Davis' scheme, Southern forces were simply to meet and repulse Federal attacks until the Union tired and called off the War. The critics, including the Richmond press, demanded a switch to an aggressive strategy. Invade the North, they urged. No less a general than Stonewall Jackson tried to persuade Lee to give the Yankees a taste of battle on their own home ground. So strongly did Jackson favor invasion that, when Lee offered him no encouragement, he went over his superior's head and made his case to President Davis — also in vain.

During that July hiatus, neither side had a clear idea of what to do next, and for good reason. The war for Virginia was now greatly expanded in scale and scope, and a delicate equilibrium existed, with the Federals' preponderance of strength balanced out by the Confederates' superior leadership. It was difficult to conceive a strategy to break the stalemate; it was easier to wait for the enemy to make an exploitable mistake.

A vague plan was stirring in the mind of Robert E. Lee. When Jackson came to him

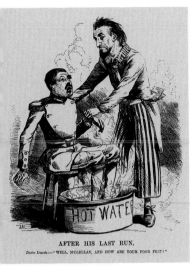

AFTER HIS LAST RUN.

Doctor Lincoln:—"WELL, McCLELLAN, AND HOW ARE YOUR POOR FEET?"

A worried Lincoln examines a sore-footed McClellan in this cartoon ridiculing the Federal retreat from the Peninsula in 1862. McClellan's failure to capture Richmond did in fact land him in political hot water, but Lincoln defended him at first, saying that his campaign was "the price we pay for the enemy not being in Washington."

to urge an invasion of the North, Lee had been too busy with urgent practical matters to spend time dreaming about remote possibilities. But he fully intended to take the offensive on a modest scale as soon as possible. He wrote: "I think we shall at least change the theater of war from the James to north of the Rappahannock. If it is effective for a season it will be a great gain."

In fact, Lee's military genius would enable him to advance against the foe more swiftly and successfully than he dared predict.

The first order of business for General Lee was to repair his battered army. Concluding that McClellan's encampment at Harrison's Landing was unassailable under the guns of U.S. warships anchored in the James, Lee on July 8 began pulling his army back toward Richmond, leaving behind only a handful of cavalrymen to warn of any menacing Federal movement. In and around Richmond, the Confederate units were refurbished with tenting and gear from captured Federal stores. There Lee undertook his main task: a thorough reorganization of his army, whose command structure had proved dangerously inadequate during the Seven Days' Battles.

No less than 11 Confederate divisions had fought in those battles. Too numerous for Lee to control in action, they tended to behave like independent armies, with little coordination between them. Lee meant to make the divisions work in harness and be more responsive to his orders.

The general realized that he could accomplish what he wanted by establishing several large commands to ensure that his orders were properly executed by their constituent units. To set up corps, however, Lee would have to circumvent a Confederate law that effectively prohibited the formation of any unit larger than a division. This law, which had been conceived primarily as a states' rights measure to maintain the authority of governors over units recruited from their states, had caused no serious difficulty until the small, scattered actions of the early War escalated into massive campaigns.

Lee began working behind the scenes to get the constraining law repealed, a goal finally achieved that November. But without waiting for official sanction, he divided his Army of Northern Virginia into two commands, which he carefully avoided calling corps. The units were sometimes referred to as "wings," but Lee preferred the entirely unspecific title "command."

Lee chose James Longstreet to lead one command and assigned him five divisions, to be headed by Major Generals Richard H. Anderson and David R. Jones, and Brigadier Generals Cadmus M. Wilcox, James L. Kemper and John Bell Hood. Lee put Jackson in charge of the second command and, perhaps because of Jackson's notorious reluctance to communicate with his subordinates, assigned him only two divisions: his own, now led by Brigadier General Charles S. Winder, and that of Richard Ewell. Lee temporarily retained under his personal direction the division of A. P. Hill. He regularized the loose but effective arrangements of his cavalry, assigning brigades to Brigadier Generals Wade Hampton, Fitzhugh Lee and Beverly H. Robertson, and placing them under the overall command of the flamboyant Jeb Stuart, now a major general.

Along with these structural changes, Lee reappraised his commanders down to the brigade level and weeded out those he considered inadequate or ill-suited to a flexible, hard-hitting army. John Magruder, who most recently had ordered useless marches at Frayser's Farm and lost his way en route to Malvern Hill, was transferred to the West. So were the aging, ineffective commanders Theophilus Holmes and Benjamin Huger.

Through it all, Lee repeatedly had to act as peacemaker in quarrels between certain proud and hot-tempered generals whom he wanted to keep. Perhaps the most sensational dispute was touched off when the Richmond *Examiner* published a glowing account of A. P. Hill's action at Frayser's Farm. Longstreet, Hill's superior in that battle, took offense and had his adjutant write a rejoinder for the rival Richmond *Whig.* The article so incensed Hill that he refused to speak with Longstreet, who thereupon had him arrested for insubordination. When they proceeded to arrange a duel, Lee interceded and stopped the fight.

Lee was not by nature a patient man, yet he now had the self-control to play a waiting game. His desire to quiet his temperamental generals and to test his revamped army did not prompt him to rush into battle. He kept watching for an enemy attack, and for the right time and place to launch his own modest offensive.

Though the Federal forces in Virginia outnumbered the Confederates by nearly 2 to 1 and were much better equipped, they faced a reorganization that was far more difficult than Lee's. And a large part of the difficulty was that President Lincoln had no general he trusted as Jefferson Davis trusted Lee.

The central question for Lincoln and Secretary of War Edwin Stanton was what to do with McClellan and his army. If McClellan would renew his drive toward Richmond,

and if at the same time a Federal attack could be mounted from the north, Lee's army might well be trapped and crushed in the huge pincers. But if McClellan would not make a timely assault, the only alternatives would be to replace him or to remove his army down the Peninsula to Fort Monroe and thence by boat up Chesapeake Bay.

McClellan did nothing to help Lincoln make up his mind. In his usual way, he greatly overestimated the enemy's strength and repeatedly bombarded Washington with excessive requests for replacements and reinforcements. "I need 50,000 more men," he had wired on July 1, "and with them I will retrieve our fortunes." Two days later he raised his requisition to 100,000 more troops, begging the President to "be fully impressed by the magnitude of the crisis in which we are placed."

Lincoln responded almost plaintively to McClellan's first request: "Allow me to reason with you a moment." Patiently the President explained that reinforcements in the numbers McClellan demanded did not exist. "If you have the impression that I blame you for not doing more than you can," Lincoln assured the general, "please be relieved of such impression. I only beg that in a like manner you will not ask impossibilities of me. If you think you are not strong enough to take Richmond just now, I do not ask you to try just now. Save the army, material and personnel, and I will strengthen it for the offensive as fast as I can."

In fact, Lincoln had already come to grips with the problem of raising more troops, a difficulty that had been exacerbated by Secretary Stanton. Back in April, while the North waxed euphoric over victories at Shiloh and elsewhere in the West, Stanton had made the dramatic and foolhardy gesture of closing the recruiting offices. In order to reopen them without appearing to panic over McClellan's costly campaign on the Peninsula, the President resorted to political maneuvering, at which he was a master. He had Secretary of State William Seward draft an appeal in the name of the 16 Northern Governors; the petition asked Lincoln to authorize the states to provide 300,000 volunteers for the "speedy restoration of the Union." Seward presented the appeal to each of the Governors at a meeting in New York City, and to a man they patriotically signed.

Of course it would take months to train and organize the 300,000 new recruits and bring them into battle. In the meantime, Lincoln and Stanton called upon help of another sort, in the form of two highly regarded generals from the West.

The first of these to arrive was Major General John Pope, who reached Washington toward the end of June. An impressive figure of a man — tall and burly, with a long beard — Pope was credited with fine work in the Federal victories at New Madrid and Island No. 10 along the Mississippi. He had been summoned because he conspicuously possessed a quality McClellan seemed to lack — zest for battle.

Pope was appointed to organize and command a new force, to be called the Army of Virginia. The army was to consist chiefly of the three corps strung out to the north and west of Richmond. Irvin McDowell's corps had one division just across the Rappahannock from Fredericksburg and another near Manassas Junction. The corps of Major Generals Nathaniel Banks and John Frémont were in the Shenandoah Valley between Winchester and Middletown.

There was an unexpected consequence to Pope's appointment. Frémont, a general with a poor performance record, was so angered at the thought of serving under an officer who was junior to him that he resigned his commission. Major General Franz Sigel, an exiled German revolutionary, was given Frémont's corps. Sigel would prove a poor choice as the campaign progressed.

The second Westerner, brought to Washington late in July, was Major General Henry W. Halleck. His reputation as a distinguished military scholar had earned him the nickname "Old Brains." And he was considered a skillful administrator in his previous post as commander of an immense military district, the Department of the Mississippi,

which embraced all of the territory from the Alleghenies to the Rocky Mountains. With high hopes, Lincoln appointed Halleck general in chief of the United States Army, a post that McClellan had held from November of 1861 to March of 1862, when the President had relieved him to prepare for the Peninsular Campaign. Since then, Lincoln and Stanton had been sharing the post with great zeal, but with results so amateurish that the need for a professional was obvious.

As soon as General Pope had unpacked in Washington, he began stoking the fires of controversy over the fate of McClellan and his army. He joined Stanton's anti-McClellan cabal and disparaged McClellan immoderately in frequent talks with Lin-

Dressed in mufti, General Henry Halleck (*far right*) visits McClellan at his headquarters near Harrison's Landing in July of 1862. McClellan held a low opinion of Halleck, his immediate superior. "I do not think he ever had a correct military idea from beginning to end," McClellan once remarked.

coln. Testifying before the Republican-controlled Committee on the Conduct of the War, he criticized McClellan for his conduct of the Peninsular Campaign; Pope branded McClellan's retreat to the James an egregious blunder, since it had permitted Lee to interpose his army between McClellan's force and Washington. Despite the considerable merit of his charges, Pope's position was tainted with cynical self-interest: He stood to gain such troops and prestige as McClellan lost.

The President listened attentively to both sides in the rancorous debate and decided to go down to Harrison's Landing and appraise the situation at first hand.

Lincoln arrived on July 7 aboard the Navy steamer *Ariel*. Wrote a chaplain of a Connecticut regiment: "We were called into line and he went the rounds. I have seldom witnessed a more ludicrous sight than our worthy Chief Magistrate presented on horseback. While I lifted my cap with respect for the man raised up by God to rule our troubled times, I lowered it speedily to cover a smile that overmastered me. It did seem as though every moment the President's legs would become entangled with those of the horse and both come down together."

Yet the chaplain added: "The boys liked him, his popularity is universal." On that score, McClellan disagreed. He wrote his wife, Nellie, that Lincoln, whom he called "an old stick and of pretty poor timber at that," was received unenthusiastically by the army. "I had to order the men to cheer and they did it very feebly."

Lincoln spent the next day sounding out senior officers about the disposition of their army. Corps commanders William Franklin and Erasmus Keyes, as well as division commander John Newton and Chief Engineer John Barnard, recommended withdrawal. The other corps commanders — Fitz-John Porter, Samuel Heintzelman and Edwin Sumner — wanted to stay and attack Richmond. So did McClellan, of course, but to Lincoln's dismay the general presented no concrete strategy and continued his excessive demands for reinforcements. To make things worse, he handed Lincoln a long, annoying letter replete with advice on political as well as military matters.

Lincoln deferred a decision for two weeks after his return to Washington. Then he sent General Halleck to Harrison's Landing to assess the military situation and make it clear to McClellan that he could have no more than 20,000 reinforcements. If McClellan rejected this offer, the army would be withdrawn from the Peninsula and sent to join Pope's forces north of the Rappahannock.

Though Halleck was less than forceful in conveying Lincoln's message, McClellan soon sensed that the tide had turned against him and began negotiating desperately, modifying his demands for more troops. Eventually he agreed to attack toward Richmond with whatever reinforcements Lincoln could give him at once. But it was too late. On August 3, the President told Halleck to order McClellan to withdraw. McClellan wired back angrily: "The order will prove disastrous to our cause. Here, directly in front of this army is the heart of the rebellion. Here is the true defense of Washington; it is here on the banks of the James."

Meanwhile, General Pope had been making only slow progress in assembling his Army of Virginia. He ordered his three corps to concentrate east of the Blue Ridge Mountains in the strategic area along the Orange & Alex-

A U.S. Army drover in Virginia rounds up cattle under an order by General Pope that allowed officers to commandeer provisions from local residents. The resulting abuses led a Union general to complain that "our men now believe they have a perfect right to rob anyone they please."

andria line between Warrenton and Culpeper Court House. But his scattered units were hard to supervise and bring together.

To announce his accession to command, Pope had made a pompous proclamation to his troops in his first general order. "I have come to you from the West," the order read, "where we have always seen the backs of our enemies. Dismiss from your minds certain phrases which I am sorry to find much in vogue amongst you. I hear constantly of 'taking strong positions and holding them,' of 'lines of retreat and bases of supplies.' Let us discard such ideas. Let us look before and not behind. Success and glory are in the advance."

The men, many of whom were veterans of the tough fighting in the Shenandoah Valley against the forces of Stonewall Jackson, resented such condescending talk. Brigadier General Marsena Patrick in McDowell's corps called the proclamation "windy and insolent." Brigadier General George H. Gordon of Banks's corps complained that Pope's bluster hurt morale, causing the troops to wonder if their commander "were not a weak and silly man." Pope was laughed at. It was said that he signed his orders "Headquarters in the Saddle," which inspired soldiers to joke that Pope did not know his headquarters from his hindquarters.

As Pope was disliked by his own men, he was detested by the foe. He stirred a storm in the South by posting in occupied Virginia decrees that went well beyond the rigors of martial law. Virginians were informed that henceforth the Federals would live off the land. Citizens would be held responsible for guerrilla attacks on Federal railroads, supply bases and soldiers. Any citizen caught in the act would be summarily executed without

benefit of trial. Southerners were outraged. Robert E. Lee called Pope "the miscreant" and declared, "He ought to be suppressed."

By July 12, Pope had tired of waiting. He decided to act. He had nothing ostentatious in mind — just a follow-up to orders he had already given. But by this small step he set in motion a succession of events that would lead to one of the War's biggest battles.

Pope ordered General Banks's corps to advance to Culpeper Court House on the Orange & Alexandria Railroad. This move would threaten Gordonsville 27 miles to the southeast, and Gordonsville was a vital junction. There the Orange & Alexandria intersected with the Virginia Central line, which linked Richmond to the Shenandoah.

Banks dispatched a vanguard of cavalry under Brigadier General John P. Hatch to tear up the tracks of the Virginia Central east of Gordonsville. But instead of moving lightly and swiftly as Pope ordered, Hatch took several days to assemble artillery and supply wagons. What was meant to be a lightning strike turned into a ponderous crawl. By the time Hatch's men had inched their way to a point 10 miles from Gordonsville, Confederate troops had occupied the town in strength; the raid was called off. This uninspired performance soon cost Hatch his command. Pope replaced him with a promising Kentuckian, Brigadier General John Buford.

Those Confederate troops in Gordonsville belonged to Jackson, and their timely arrival had been the result of a daring gamble by Lee. Lee had learned of Banks's advance toward Gordonsville on July 12, the very day it began. The next morning, at the risk of leaving the Richmond defenses with less than half as many troops as McClellan commanded, Lee told Jackson to rush his two divisions

north into a blocking position. Three days later, after a frantic roundup of railroad cars, Jackson's 18,000 troops piled onto 18 trains of 15 cars each, and by the night of July 19 they were encamped at Gordonsville.

As Banks's advance stalled and Pope continued to gather his forces, Lee turned even bolder. By July 27, he made the reasoned guess that McClellan would continue to sit by harmlessly at Harrison's Landing, and he ordered A. P. Hill's Light Division — so called for its speed on the march — to join Jackson. Lee was more than a little concerned that Jackson's secretive, lone-wolf ways would anger the impetuous, hot-tempered Hill. So Lee in his most tactful manner wrote Jackson: "A. P. Hill you will find a good officer with whom you can consult and by advising with your division commanders as to their movements much trouble can be saved you." Unfortunately, Jackson chose not to heed Lee's suggestions.

On August 3, Lee received news in Richmond that told him the time was right for his limited offensive. A promising young cavalry lieutenant named John Singleton Mosby had recently arrived from Fort Monroe at the tip of the Peninsula; he had been released by

In a sketch for *Leslie's Illustrated Weekly*, Federal troops fan out to advance on Confederate-held Cedar Mountain *(left)*. The numerals on the sketch keyed the scene for the journal's editors; number 2, for example, indicates the Confederate battle line on the mountainside.

the Federals in an exchange of prisoners. Mosby told Lee that Major General Ambrose Burnside and 14,000 Federal troops, having reached the Peninsula from the Carolinas, had been ordered to move farther north by water. Mosby concluded, and Lee agreed, that Burnside was heading up Chesapeake Bay and the Potomac to reinforce Pope's troops at Aquia Landing and nearby Fredericksburg. Since that implied that McClellan was no longer a threat to Richmond, Lee gave Jackson a mandate to strike before Pope did. "I would rather you should have easy fighting and heavy victories," Lee declared. "I now leave the matter to your reflection and good judgement."

Jackson determined to march his forces to Orange Court House on August 7, cross the Rapidan the next day, and attack Pope's advance units near Culpeper.

Jackson's scheme was a good one. There was only one problem; he failed to tell his generals what he planned to do. General Ewell, who had been driven to distraction by Jackson's inscrutable ways in the Valley Campaign, was asked by a junior officer what Jackson had in mind, and he had to confess: "I do not know whether we march north, south, east or west, or whether we march at all. General Jackson has simply ordered me to have the division ready to move at dawn."

Leaving Gordonsville on the 7th, Jackson's command marched on back roads to Orange Court House and bivouacked for the night. While the troops slept, Jackson issued orders for the march along the main road to Culpeper. He wanted Ewell's division to lead off, followed by Hill's and then his own division, under General Winder. But during the night Jackson changed his mind and told

This portrait of Stonewall Jackson was one of the few photographs of the Confederate general made during the War. It was taken at Winchester in the Shenandoah Valley, where in May of 1862 Jackson defeated Nathaniel Banks, the man who was to be his opponent at Cedar Mountain.

Major General Nathaniel P. Banks, a former congressman and governor of Massachusetts, was a political appointee with little military experience. At Cedar Mountain, he may have hoped to best his nemesis Jackson by striking quickly before the latter could marshal his forces.

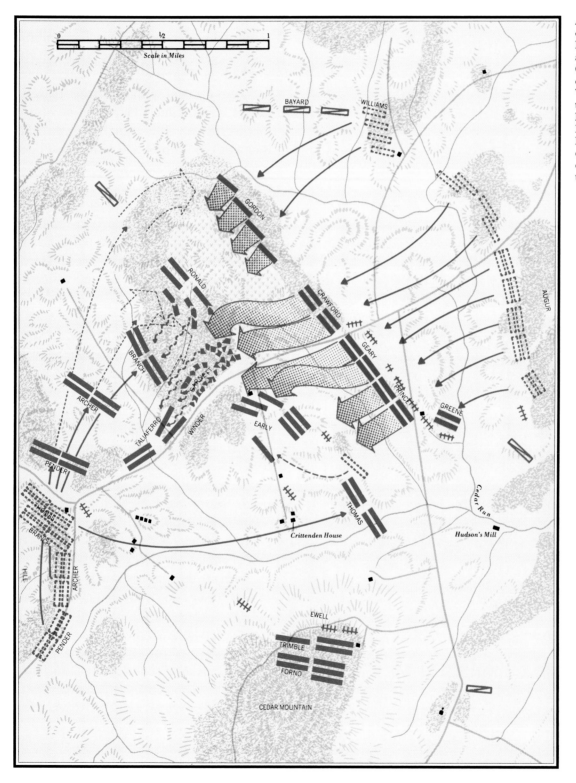

At Cedar Mountain on the afternoon of August 9, the outnumbered Federals under Nathaniel Banks attacked from a position north of Cedar Run. Crawford's brigade overwhelmed the Confederates under Winder and Taliaferro, enveloping the left side of Jackson's line. But Banks lacked reserves, and as the Federal assault petered out, A. P. Hill's fresh Confederate division came up and delivered a crushing counterattack that drove Banks's troops from the field.

Ewell to take a different route, one that veered west before rejoining the Culpeper road to the north. In his usual mystifying way, Jackson failed to inform Hill or Winder. The next morning, August 8, Hill and his men waited patiently as troops began to pass by. But instead of being Ewell's men, they were Winder's.

Hill was furious. He was also in a quandary over what to do. So as not to mix the units, he decided to hold back his division until all of Winder's men and wagons had passed. The result was a costly delay. Winder's men made only four miles that day, and Hill's division, after finally getting on the road and marching two miles, was ordered back to Orange Court House for the night. Ewell, having escaped the mix-up, easily made eight miles, but except for that the day had been wasted. Jackson blamed Hill for the delay; Hill blamed Jackson.

This contretemps turned out to be less damaging than it might have been. Pope, who had left Washington to join his army in the field on July 29, was still having trouble concentrating his forces between Culpeper and Warrenton. More than half of McDowell's 30,000-man corps was still at Fredericksburg. Sigel's 13,000-man corps was slowly making its way from the Valley across the Blue Ridge. Only Banks, with 11,000 men, was in position.

All this made General Halleck exceedingly nervous. He wired Pope: "Do not advance so as to expose yourself to any disaster, unless you can better your line of defense, until we can get more troops upon the Rappahannock." He also prodded McClellan with a wire on August 7, the day after the Army of the Potomac had begun its ponderous withdrawal. "I must beg of you, general, to hurry along your movement. Your reputation as well as mine may be involved in its rapid execution. I cannot regard Pope and Burnside as safe until you reinforce them."

By August 8, Pope's infantry was strung out for 20 miles along the road from Sperryville, at the foot of the Blue Ridge, to a point just south of Culpeper. His cavalry was stretched from Madison Court House to Rapidan Station. One of McDowell's divisions, under Brigadier General Rufus King, remained at Fredericksburg to guard the approaches to the Federal supply base at Aquia Landing, where Burnside's corps was soon to arrive. Sigel, who had been ordered to march rapidly from Sperryville, had misread his maps and led his corps off track. Another of McDowell's divisions, under Brigadier General James B. Ricketts, was at Culpeper. In the vanguard of Pope's army, about eight miles south of Culpeper, was the corps commanded by Nathaniel Banks.

On August 9, Jackson's Confederates moved north, with Ewell's division in the lead, followed by Winder's. Hill pushed his men hard to close the gap created by the confusion of the preceding day. Once the three divisions had linked up, they formed a column of 24,000 men and 1,200 wagons stretching for seven miles. The cavalry, under Beverly Robertson, screened the march, steadily pushing back Federal cavalry scouts. It was hot even in the early morning hours. As the temperature rose to near 100 degrees, many men dropped of sunstroke. Winder had been taken ill, but was carried in an ambulance alongside his men.

Shortly after noon, a courier informed Jackson that the head of the column had encountered Federals "in strong force" on the Culpeper road. Jackson rode forward to con-

The Charmed Life of a Durable Artillerist

Major Richard Snowden Andrews, the 31-year-old commander of General Winder's divisional artillery, was still recovering from an injury received during the Seven Days' Battles when he led his batteries into action against the Federals at Cedar Mountain on August 9, 1862. There, near the front, a Federal shell struck his right side, ripping a gaping hole in his stomach and nearly disemboweling him.

With remarkable presence of mind, Andrews clasped his intestines in one hand and slid from his horse so that he rolled to the ground on his back. There he lay for three hours until an ambulance took him to a field hospital.

The Army surgeons, on seeing Andrews' condition, declared that there was no hope: Even if the wound could be closed, a fatal infection would surely follow. Told that his chances were less than one in a hundred, Andrews replied: "Well, I am going to hold on to my one chance."

A surgeon then cut away Andrews' jacket, washed the wound and sewed him up crudely with a needle and thread. Andrews was placed on a bed, and the next day his wife hurried to his side, bringing with her a skilled physician and the newborn baby he had not yet seen.

Miraculously, no infection developed. Within two months, Andrews was able to hobble around on crutches. Eight months later, wearing a special metal plate over his wound to protect it, he rejoined his unit — just in time to be wounded again on the way to Gettysburg.

After a second painful convalescence, Andrews was discharged and assigned as a Confederate envoy to Europe. At War's end, he returned to his native Baltimore, where he lived peacefully for three more decades until his death at the age of 73.

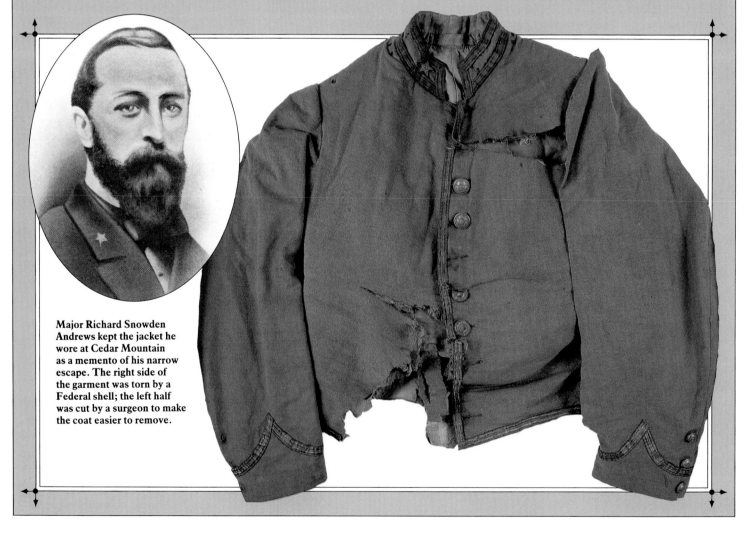

Major Richard Snowden Andrews kept the jacket he wore at Cedar Mountain as a memento of his narrow escape. The right side of the garment was torn by a Federal shell; the left half was cut by a surgeon to make the coat easier to remove.

fer with Ewell. As he did so, Federal artillery opened up on Ewell's lead brigade. This unit, under the command of Brigadier General Jubal A. Early, was then marching along the western slope of Cedar Mountain, a low, mile-long ridge.

Jackson, moving quickly to secure the dominant terrain of Cedar Mountain (*map, page 100*), ordered Ewell to anchor his artillery on the northern end of the mountain. Ewell deployed Early's brigade to face the center of the Federal line, arrayed behind a ridge to the north of Cedar Run. On the far right, at the foot of Cedar Mountain, Ewell stationed the brigades commanded by Brigadier General Issac Trimble and Colonel Henry Forno.

Next to come up was Charles Winder, who left his ambulance against doctor's orders and positioned his division to the left of Ewell, covering what appeared to be the Federal right. In a potentially fatal oversight, two Union brigades went undetected opposite the Confederate left flank. The Federals were concealed in thick woods beyond a wheat field northwest of the Culpeper road. Nearby, in woods alongside the road, stood Winder's Second and Third Brigades under Colonel Thomas Garnett and Brigadier General William Taliaferro, with the famed Stonewall Brigade, led by Colonel Charles Ronald, held in reserve. Since Jackson anticipated action to his right, the Confederates along the road were facing southeast — away from the unseen enemy.

By midafternoon, Ewell's and Winder's lines stretched from the northern tip of Cedar Mountain to the woods along the Culpeper road. To the rear lay Hill's Light Division, ready to move in any direction.

At that juncture, the Federals were greatly outnumbered by Jackson's command. Only one complete Federal corps, Banks's, was on hand to meet the threat. On his left, facing Ewell, Banks had the three brigades of Major General Christopher Augur's division. On the Federal right, across the road, were the two brigades of Major General Alpheus Williams' division. Brigadier General Samuel W. Crawford's 1,700 men, concealed in the thick woods beyond the wheat field, were closest to the enemy, while Brigadier General George Gordon's troops held positions to Crawford's right and rear. Though other units were coming up, the Federals had no more than 9,000 men immediately available — about 12,000 less than the Confederates. Yet in spite of that, orders were issued that led to a Federal attack.

Early that morning, Pope had dispatched one of his aides, Colonel Louis Marshall — a nephew of Robert E. Lee — with verbal orders for Banks at his Culpeper headquarters. According to Banks, Marshall gave him instructions to "assume command of all the forces in the front, deploy his skirmishers if the enemy approaches, and attack him immediately as soon as he approaches." Banks then left Culpeper for the field, and his artillery went into action as soon as Jackson's vanguard came within range.

By 4:30 that afternoon, cannon fire on both sides had intensified. Ewell's batteries at the mountain and Winder's on the left drew heavy and accurate fire from the ridge north of Cedar Run. Winder's chief of artillery, Major Richard Snowden Andrews, was hit and gravely wounded as he tried to move some smoothbores toward the front. Winder himself was standing behind one of his batteries, selecting targets for his gunners, when a bursting shell mangled his left arm

Led by Brigadier General Samuel Crawford, Federal troops roll up the left flank of Jackson's army at Cedar Mountain, routing two regiments of the celebrated Stonewall Brigade. The tough Confederate veterans had never before been driven from the field, and their retreat nearly cost Jackson the battle.

and ripped open his left side. As Winder's staff officers tried frantically to get him medical aid, a rider galloped through the trees with an urgent message from Early; a Federal column had been spotted on their extreme left, beyond Garnett's brigade. Winder was carried to the rear; the brave and talented Marylander would die that evening of his wounds. Command of his division devolved upon Taliaferro, who was completely ignorant of Jackson's battle plan.

When Jackson was informed of Winder's mortal wound, he hurried to Garnett's brigade, the northernmost Confederate unit. The general warned Garnett to watch out for his exposed left flank. Taliaferro received no warning, but he spotted the Federal column to his left and made a desperate attempt to pivot his defense line to face the threat from the northwest.

Suddenly, at 5 p.m., Crawford's Federals emerged from the far woods. Flags flying and bayonets glistening, they came charging through the newly cut wheat field, dotted with neat shocks. Although Taliaferro's brigade was not yet prepared to make a strong stand against the onrushing enemy, Garnett's Confederates to the north managed to unleash some deadly volleys. Still, three of Crawford's regiments — the 46th Pennsylvania, 28th New York and 5th Connecticut — crossed a rail fence, charged into the woods along the road and caved in three successive Confederate lines.

Hand-to-hand fighting raged through the woods. Little quarter was asked or given. A Federal officer shot down six opponents with his revolver. Lieutenant Thomas W. Brown of the 21st Virginia was knocked down and fatally bayoneted after surrendering. Before long, all three of the brigades along the Cul-

105

peper road were put to rout, including the vaunted Stonewall Brigade, which had been caught up in the assault. Confederate artillerymen limbered up their guns and galloped to the rear to escape capture. The entire left wing of Jackson's command had been outflanked and unhinged.

At almost the same time, Early's brigade was being turned by Augur's Federals, who had moved down the Culpeper road and deployed in open fields opposite the Confederate right.

A rider raced back to Jackson with the grim news. Alarmed, Jackson galloped to the front through heavy cannonading and past shattered regiments streaming to the rear. He jerked a battle flag from a color-bearer's hand, waved it above his head and shouted, "Rally, brave men, and press forward! Your general will lead you. Jackson will lead you. Follow me!"

At this point, Jackson made a gesture that would long delight his admirers. Returning the flag to the color-bearer, he reached down to draw his sword. As it happened, Jackson so rarely drew his sword that it had rusted into its scabbard. No matter. Quickly, Jackson unhooked the scabbard,

Because of ill health, Brigadier General Charles S. Winder was urged by Stonewall Jackson's physician to take no part in the battle at Cedar Mountain; he ignored the advice and was killed by a Federal shell. The normally stoic Jackson was stunned by the loss of his most trusted subordinate. He wrote that he could hardly think of Winder's death "without tearful eyes."

Lines of horse-drawn ambulance wagons come and go outside a farmhouse the Federals used as a field hospital during the Battle of Cedar Mountain. An artillery duel rages in the distance.

waved the sheathed sword over his head and led his men forward.

"Jackson usually is an indifferent and slouchy looking man, but his whole person changed," one of the Confederates recalled after the battle. "His face was lit with the inspiration of heroism. Even the old sorrel horse seemed endowed with the form of an Arabian."

As defeated units rallied and their officers regained control, Jackson galloped back to the rear to urge A. P. Hill's division into the battle. The first troops he encountered were those commanded by Brigadier General Lawrence O'Bryan Branch, a former congressman from North Carolina. Jackson found Branch making a speech to his brigade and, according to one account, quickly cut him short. "Push forward, general," Jackson snapped, "push forward!"

Branch later offered a somewhat different account of his superior's arrival. "General Jackson came to me and told me his left was beaten and broken, and the enemy was turning him and he wished me to advance. I was already in the line of battle and instantly gave the order, 'Forward, march!' I had not gone 100 yards through the woods before we met the celebrated Stonewall Brigade, utterly routed and fleeing as fast as they could run."

Branch's men pushed ahead and soon ran into some of Crawford's Federals, racing in hot pursuit of the Stonewall Brigade. After a brief melee, the Federal troops were pushed back through the woods along the road and into the open wheat field.

As Branch's battle line moved forward into the wheat field, General Jackson again rode up. "I reported my brigade as being solid," Branch remembered, "and asked for orders. My men recognized him and raised a terrific shout as he rode along the line with his hat off."

By now, the rest of Hill's 12,000-man division was reaching the front. Brigade by brigade, they advanced into battle. Though Federal reinforcements were on the way from Culpeper, they would arrive much too late to save Crawford's brigade. "The reserves of the enemy were thrown upon the broken ranks," Crawford later wrote. "The field-officers had all been killed, wounded or taken prisoners; the support I looked for did not arrive, and my gallant men, broken, decimated by that fearful fire, that unequal contest, fell back across the space, leaving most of their number upon the field." Color Sergeant James Hewison of the 5th Connecticut, twice wounded but determined to prevent his state flag from being captured, tore the banner from its staff, wrapped it around him and crawled back to his own lines.

By the time the survivors disengaged, Crawford's ill-fated brigade had lost nearly 50 per cent of its strength — 494 men killed or wounded and 373 missing. One regiment, the 28th New York, lost 17 of its 18 officers.

Despite the terrible toll, some Federals on Banks's crumbling right flank still beat desperately against the Confederate counterattack. Brigadier General George Bayard ordered a squadron of the 1st Pennsylvania Cavalry to charge straight into Branch's oncoming battle line. Of the 164 Federal horsemen, all but 71 were killed or wounded. But their bravery bought enough time for the infantry and artillery to fall back, rally and resume the fight.

The Union's General Gordon advanced his brigade into the wheat field to cover

Crawford's retreat. Most of Gordon's units were driven back. But the men of the 2nd Massachusetts held. Outnumbered 3 to 1, they put up a stiff fight under their West Point commander, Colonel George L. Andrews, and an elite officer staff composed chiefly of Harvard graduates. Then, as one of Hill's brigades struck the regiment's right flank, the Massachusetts men were caught in a deadly cross fire. Wrote Lieutenant Charles F. Morse, "The roar of musketry was perfectly deafening; the noise of the bullets through the air was like a gale of wind; our poor men were dropping on every side—it seemed as if only a miracle could save anyone." Their heavy losses not withstanding, the 2nd Massachusetts was one of the last Federal units to retreat that day.

Late in the afternoon, General Hill prepared to lead the final Confederate assault. He took off his jacket, revealing the red battle shirt that identified him to his troops.

Then he drew his saber and waved his men forward all along the line from the woods north of the wheat field to the Culpeper road. The Federal line crumbled and gave way. By 6:30, after little over an hour of bloody action, the victory was complete.

Jackson still was not satisfied; he ordered Hill to continue the chase. But darkness and exhaustion slowed the Confederates, and at last, as they advanced to within seven miles of Culpeper, their drive was brought to a halt by a fresh division of Federal troops under General Ricketts. Sometime after 11 p.m., Jackson decided to hazard no more in the darkness and ordered the troops to bivouac on the ground.

Wrote Jackson's Chief of Staff, Major Robert L. Dabney: "Jackson gathered his wearied staff about him, and rode languidly back through the field of strife, lately so stormy, but now silent, save where the groans of the wounded broke the stillness.

Under a flag of truce, Federal and Confederate soldiers remove their dead and wounded from the field after the Battle of Cedar Mountain. Although the terms of the cease-fire allowed the troops only to tend to the casualties, Jackson's men also retrieved more than 1,000 Federal muskets and side arms left on the battlefield. Federal officers protested vigorously, but were loath to renew the fighting.

He observed a little grass plot, and declared that he could go no farther. A cloak was spread for him upon the ground, when he prostrated himself on it upon his breast, and in a moment forgot his toils and fatigues in deep slumber."

In his account of the clash at Cedar Mountain, a Northern reporter found merit on both sides: "The valor of the combatants was unquestionable." But it was an ugly little battle, badly mismanaged on both sides. It cost Jackson 1,355 men killed and wounded, while Banks suffered 2,377 casualties— nearly 30 per cent of his corps.

Banks later denied that he had ordered the costly premature attack. Pope claimed that he had intended Banks to stay on the defensive until General Sigel's corps arrived. In any case, Pope had contributed heavily to the confusion by sending Colonel Marshall to Banks with verbal orders that were easily misunderstood.

General Jackson had not done much better. His orders had been vague, and the day he lost in the confused march from Gordonsville gave Banks a chance to improve his position. Once the battle was joined at Cedar Mountain, Jackson failed to anticipate the danger on his left and made a faulty disposition of his forces; his men had to fight furiously to redeem the situation against a greatly outnumbered foe.

Still, Lee's cautious but opportunistic leadership was beginning to produce results. Though his army was still being reorganized, he had indeed taken the fight to the enemy. Now new offensive vistas opened up to Robert E. Lee.

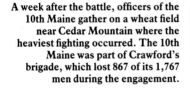

A week after the battle, officers of the 10th Maine gather on a wheat field near Cedar Mountain where the heaviest fighting occurred. The 10th Maine was part of Crawford's brigade, which lost 867 of its 1,767 men during the engagement.

Federal artillerymen ford a tributary of the Rappahannock on August 9, 1862, the day Nathaniel Banks's corps of Pope's army was defeated at Cedar Mountain.

On the Move with Pope's Army

Not long after the Battle of Cedar Mountain on August 9, 1862, the weary, dispirited troops of General John Pope's Army of Virginia were forced to withdraw by the threat of a Confederate flanking movement. Already discouraged by their defeat at the hands of Stonewall Jackson's men, they were further demoralized by the hardships of their strenuous march northward. With them was a New York photographer named Timothy O'Sullivan, who captured these candid views of life in Pope's army before and after Cedar Mountain.

"Our tired, sleepy men were in poor condition for the long, hot, dusty march," wrote one of Pope's brigade commanders. But march the troops did, so hard and so fast that many regiments soon outstripped their supply and baggage wagons. "My blankets and overcoat are with the baggage train which is heaven knows where, and which we shall see again no one knows when," a Massachusetts soldier complained in a letter to his parents. "For a week we have slept on the ground, and for two days had almost nothing to eat."

To make matters worse, the retreat was punctuated by frequent skirmishes with the enemy — at a time when many Federals were almost too weak to fight. Men of the 60th New York had been stricken with typhoid fever several weeks before the retreat. "Nearly all of us were more or less debilitated, and needed quiet and nursing," recalled the regiment's chaplain. "We were therefore somewhat surprised when, instead of the rest we had expected, we found ourselves drawn up in line of battle."

Before the advance to Cedar Mountain, Federal officers visit with their families at a field hospital in Manassas, Virginia.

In the blazing July heat, Federal soldiers loll in a grassy field not far from Bull Run and share a simple meal.

A photographer at Manassas — probably Timothy O'Sullivan — stops for a drink beside his mobile darkroom.

The heaviest of the fighting during the Battle of Cedar Mountain took place around this gently rolling wheat field about a mile from the mountain proper.

Bloated carcasses of horses litter the field at Cedar Mountain. By the time this picture was taken, several days after the battle, most of the men killed had been buried.

This modest dwelling near the Cedar Mountain battlefield was used as a Confederate hospital; the well in the foreground provided water for the wounded.

Confederates captured at Cedar Mountain hang their laundry from the balcony of Culpeper Court House, where the Federals housed prisoners before the retreat.
116

A Federal freight train pulls into the Culpeper station, a crucial depot along Pope's line of retreat.

Federal soldiers encamped in the village of Culpeper take their ease as curious civilians look on.

Retreating before the Confederate pursuit from the south, Federal supply wagons cross a railroad bridge over the Rappahannock. Soldiers had covered the ties wit

…lanks to enable horses and vehicles to negotiate the span; the catwalk below may have been for the use of foot soldiers when the span was jammed with traffic.

Using a block and tackle to hoist logs into place, Federal soldiers repair a bridge destroyed by the Confederates.

Officers of the 60th New York pause for photographer O'Sullivan at Fauquier Sulphur Springs before joining the general retreat.

The sleepy town of Warrenton, pictured here in August of 1862, lay in the path of Pope's Federals as they marched north.

Federal soldiers survey the wreckage of a train demolished by General Stonewall Jackson's troops during a surprise attack on Manassas Junction on August 26. By the

tion and to reinforcements arriving from Alexandria — and Lee was quick to exploit its vulnerability.

At the moment, Lee had about the same number of men as Pope, which the Confederate general considered good odds. Lee's plan called for Stuart's cavalry to demolish the railroad bridge over the Rappahannock, cutting Pope off from his base of supply. At the same time Lee, moving behind the cover of Clark's Mountain, east of the railroad, would cross the Rapidan and attack Pope's left flank, smashing him before McClellan's reinforcements arrived. All this was better in theory than in practice, however. Logistical problems delayed Lee's offensive for two crucial days. Then the redoubtable Jeb Stuart was surprised and almost captured by a detachment of Federal cavalry. Stuart spurred his horse over a fence, leaving behind his famed plumed hat in the rush. One of Stuart's staff officers, Captain Norman Fitzhugh, was not so fortunate. He was captured, and in his dispatch case the Federals discovered an order outlining Lee's plan. When Pope learned of the impending Confederate attack, he immediately ordered his army north of the Rappahannock.

The Federals moved rapidly. "The heat was intense and the dust suffocating," wrote Chaplain William Locke of the 11th Pennsylvania, but the troops made haste, convinced that "grim and relentless as fate, the rebel hordes were already on our trail and eager for our destruction." The Virginia citizenry welcomed the retreat. At Culpeper, Locke saw a little dark-eyed girl swinging aloft a bonnet. She cried after them, "Goodbye, Yankees. I'm glad you're going."

On August 20, Confederate cavalry pursuing Pope's army clashed with Federal troopers under Brigadier General George Bayard. Though the Federals got the worst of it, the 26-year-old Bayard bought enough time for the tail of Pope's column to cross the Rappahannock. When Lee's soldiers reached the river a day later, they found the opposite heights well manned by troops ready to dispute any crossing. Lee made several exploratory stabs, but the opposite bank of the Rappahannock was consistently higher than the near bank, and wherever Lee probed, men and guns were looking down on him. Time was leaking away.

On August 22, Stuart took 1,500 cavalrymen and two guns, rode far upstream and crossed the unguarded Waterloo Bridge. He then skirted Pope's flank, intending to cut the Orange & Alexandria Railroad to the north. Charging out of a raging thunderstorm on what Stuart remembered as "the darkest night I ever saw," the Confederate horsemen struck the Federal camp at Catlett's Station, on the railroad 10 miles behind the Federal lines. Only when he arrived did Stuart learn that this also was Pope's headquarters. Pope was away and the nearby railroad bridge over Cedar Run was too wet to burn and too stout to chop down, but Stuart managed to seize Pope's dress uniform — some compensation for his hat — along with Pope's dispatch case.

As Pope had read Lee's mail, Lee now read his — and found the news bad. The first contingents of McClellan's troops were near at hand. Fitz-John Porter's V Corps had arrived at Aquia Landing, off the Potomac, on August 22. Though Porter's artillery was in disarray — horses on one ship, guns on another — and his infantrymen had only 40 cartridges apiece, he was moving west quickly to join Pope. Heintzelman's III Corps, which lacked artillery altogether, was landing at Alexandria and would soon move southward, followed by Franklin's VI Corps. Soon Pope would have 70,000 men. The time already was past for a head-on attack across the Rappahannock.

Lee then made another decision that was breathtaking in its audacity—one so risky that for a long time the Federal command refused to believe that he would do such a thing and thus was slow to respond. Though military dogma called for concentrating one's force when faced with an enemy of superior numbers, Lee decided to *divide* his small army. He would send Jackson with 25,000 men, including Stuart's cavalry, in a great circle to the north of Pope while Longstreet's 30,000 demonstrated on the Rappahannock to conceal the move.

Maneuvers toward Washington invariably stirred Union fears, and Lee was sure that Pope, when threatened by the flanking move, would fall back to cover his line to the capital. The day after Jackson left, Longstreet would follow on the same circuitous route to the north. The two forces would then reunite and strike Pope a mighty blow while he was off balance. The effect would be to move Pope farther from Richmond and to deprive him of his strong position on the Rappahannock. There was little time, but Lee still hoped to demolish Pope before McClellan's troops came up in force.

The plan was hazardous in the extreme. If Pope grasped Lee's intentions, he could move his army to keep the two elements separated and then destroy them one at a time. One of Lee's officers wrote later: "We have record of few enterprises of greater daring. To risk cause and country, name and reputation, on a single throw and to abide the issue

with unflinching heart is the supreme exhibit of the soldier's fortitude."

On the afternoon of August 24, Lee conferred with Jackson. Captain Henry Kyd Douglas, Jackson's young aide, recalled the meeting—at a table set in a field. Lee, Stuart and Longstreet sat and Jackson stood, while staff officers remained out of earshot on a nearby knoll. As Douglas approached the table, Jackson was saying, "I shall move within an hour." He would have his army ready to march at dawn, by which Jackson meant scarcely after midnight. They would travel light, with three days' cooked rations in their haversacks. There would be artillery, ammunition wagons, ambulances and a herd of beef cattle. The time was so short, said Private John Worsham of the 21st Virginia, "that none of the men had cooked all and many none of their rations" when ordered to fall in and start the march.

Pope soon was aware of Jackson's advance. By 8 a.m. on August 25, Federal signal stations on hilltops along the Rappahannock were reporting the enemy movement with an accurate count of numbers based on regimental flags. But the question was, where were they going? Pope suspected that they were headed for the Shenandoah Valley, scene of Jackson's old successes, and surmised that Lee's whole army would follow. The only trouble with this thesis was that Longstreet remained in place along the Rappahannock making a conspicuous demonstration, as he put it later, "to impress Pope with the idea that I was attempting to force a passage at his front." During this busy, confusing day, the possibility that Jackson might be making for the Federal rear seems not to have occurred to Pope.

Jackson rode along his column. "Close

Catlett's Station, General John Pope's headquarters on the Orange & Alexandria Railroad just 30 miles south of Washington, was struck by Jeb Stuart's cavalry in a night raid on August 22, 1862. The troopers made off with $350,000 in cash as well as Pope's dispatch book and cloak.

up, men," he repeated, "close up." Many of the troops were veterans of the grueling Valley marches, and they moved northwestward with steady rhythm along the Rappahannock, upriver to Amissville, across to Orleans, on toward Salem. Here and there, farmers and townfolk came out with biscuits, cold chicken and ham, and buckets of cool well water. Jackson, closemouthed as always, told no one their destination, and rumors flew up and down the line. Was it back to the Valley again?

The road was stony and many men were barefoot. Lieutenant Colonel Edward McCrady of the 1st South Carolina remembered the bloodstains left in the dirt by shoeless men. Later he would see raw blisters on the still bare feet of men who lay dead on the battlefield.

"Clouds of choking dust enveloped the hurrying column," Allen C. Redwood of the 55th Virginia remembered, "but on and on the march was pushed without relenting. Haversacks were empty by noon and the column subsisted itself upon green corn and apples from the fields along the route, devoured while marching. It was far on in the night when the column stopped and the weary men dropped beside their stacked muskets and were instantly asleep, without so much as unrolling a blanket."

In the night, Redwood recalled, the men "were shaken up again and limped on in the darkness only half-awake. There was no mood for speech — only the shuffling tramp of the marching feet, the steady rumbling of wheels, the creak and rattle and clank of harness with an occasional order uttered under

the breath and always the same: 'Close up. Close up, men.' "

Then at Salem they turned east, paralleling the Manassas Gap Railroad, and Jackson's troops knew where they were going. Behind them lay the Blue Ridge; up ahead were the Bull Run Mountains and Thoroughfare Gap, which led to the plain of Manassas and the railroad junction where Pope's vast supply depot lay. The question rippled along the line: Did Federals await them at the gap? It was a narrow gash in the wooded ridge, with steep, rocky sides. A relatively small force could hold it long enough for couriers to warn Pope so that his army could move back. Then the answer passed down the line like a hurrah: The gap was open. There was not a Federal in sight, and the lead elements were already through and descending undetected on Pope's rear.

That Pope would neglect to guard a natural route to the rear of his army seemed incredible. In fact, he knew the route was open, but he was sure it would not be used. He had made up his mind: Jackson was moving to the Shenandoah Valley.

At midmorning on August 26, Jackson reached Gainesville and turned southeast toward Bristoe Station, where the Orange & Alexandria crossed Broad Run. This was a full 20 miles behind Pope's line on the Rappahannock. Now, recalled Captain William Blackford, one of Stuart's staff officers attached to Jackson's command, "the troops began to show the effects of the hard labor and of the heat. Many fainted and great numbers became footsore." Late that afternoon the Confederate vanguard reached Bristoe Station, overwhelmed the two Federal companies there and cut the telegraph line.

Then the Confederates heard a whistle:

A train was approaching from the south, bound for Alexandria to pick up supplies for Pope's army. The men threw ties across the track, but the train shoved them aside and sped away in a storm of bullets, carrying the alarm. Prisoners taken at the station said more empty trains would be along soon, and several Confederates tore up a rail on the embankment. The next train approached, took a volley in passing from men of the Louisiana Brigade and ran into the break in the tracks.

"Down the embankment rushed the engine, screaming and hissing," wrote Captain Blackford, "and down upon it rushed the cars, piling up one upon another until the pile reached higher than the embankment." The train's rear cars remained on the track, and as darkness fell another train came on at full speed and crashed into the wreck. "The locomotive plowed under the first three boxcars, setting them crossways on its back and on the back of the tender. The cars telescoped each other and many were forced out upon the pile over the locomotive." Within the hour, a fourth train came along. It screeched to a halt and backed down the track.

Jackson sent a detail to burn the trestle over Broad Run, north of the station, and began interrogating the surviving trainmen. He had a fire kindled for light and stood outlined against it, a gaunt figure in dusty clothes, slope-shouldered and slouched, an old forage cap drawn down to his nose. Across the way a Union civilian with a broken leg asked to be raised so he could see this scourge of the Federal Army. He gazed in amazement and dismay — and groaned, "Oh, my God! Lay me down." The comment ran through the army, and though Jackson never quite understood its deriva-

Pillaging Pope's supply depot at Manassas Junction on August 27, Stonewall Jackson's troops help themselves to a Federal cornucopia of food and equipment. "For a change of underclothing and a pot of French mustard," wrote one of the raiders, "I owe grateful thanks to the major of the 12th Pennsylvania Cavalry."

tion — or its humor — for months thereafter his men greeted every privation or disaster with the cry, "Oh, my God! Lay me down."

Jackson's army, having marched 56 miles in two days, was worn out. But the Federal supply depot at Manassas Junction lay just four miles to the north. Jackson sent old Isaac Trimble, a brigadier general who was always ready for a fight, out with the 21st Georgia and the 21st South Carolina.

The attackers approached their target quietly at midnight. The supply depot was guarded only by a couple of batteries and a handful of men. The gunners managed to get off one salvo, but before they could reload, the Confederates were on them. "Give 'em another round boys, it's only some damned guerrillas," cried a Federal artillery officer in the dark. A pistol appeared at his ear. "I reckon, Colonel, you have got in the wrong crowd," drawled a Georgia private.

His way thus prepared, Jackson left Richard Ewell with three brigades to guard Bristoe Station and moved the bulk of his army to Manassas. The men stumbled through the night like specters, wrote Redwood, "gaunt-cheeked and hollow-eyed, hair, beard, clothing covered with dust." But when dawn broke over Manassas, they saw a sight that lifted their hearts and banished exhaustion.

The supply depot covered nearly a square mile. Two rail sidings, each a half mile long, were lined with loaded boxcars. There were sheds, warehouses, stacks of ammunition,

Though inept as a general, German-born Franz Sigel rallied thousands of fellow immigrants to the Union cause. Among the units he led at Bull Run in 1862 was the company below, part of the all-German 41st New York. An officer noted that the "excitable" Sigel had some "hardheaded, common-sense men with him who will save him from disaster."

tarpaulin-covered piles of foodstuffs. There were sutler's wagons full of luxuries, including fine wines and expensive cigars. All this was spread before men who had been living for days mainly on green corn and apples. Private Worsham remembered "vast storehouses filled with all the delicacies, potted ham, lobster, tongue, candy, cakes, nuts, oranges, lemons, pickle, catsup, mustard, etc. It makes an old soldier's mouth water now just to think of it. Some filled their haversacks with cakes, some with candy, others with oranges, lemons, canned goods, etc. I know one that took nothing but French mustard; it turned out to be the best thing taken, as he traded it for meat and bread, it lasting him for days."

Private William McClendon of the 15th Alabama was practical. He teamed with Barnett Cody of his regiment, loading a 25-pound side of bacon in a knapsack while Cody packed 20 pounds of hardtack crackers. They added all the coffee and sugar they could carry and were ready for the future. Captain Blackford found a new saddle, and other men got new shoes and boots, shirts and britches, underwear and blankets. "Fine whiskey and segars circulated freely," Blackford wrote, "elegant linen hankerchiefs were applied to noses hitherto blown by the thumb and forefinger, and sumptuous underclothing was fitted over limbs sunburnt, sore and vermin-splotched."

On one score, Jackson took no chances. Major W. Roy Mason remembered that the general's first order was "to knock out the heads of hundreds of barrels of whiskey, wine, brandy. I shall never forget the scene. Streams of spirits ran like water through the sands of Manassas and the soldiers on hands and knees drank it greedily from the

131

ground." An Alabamian recalled Jackson's comment: "I fear that whiskey more than I do Pope's army."

In that day of plunder, the only Federal troops to engage Jackson's force at Manassas did so by accident. That morning, the New Jersey Brigade, part of the reinforcements from Franklin's corps, arrived by train at the bridge over Bull Run, about five miles north of Manassas Junction. Brigadier General George W. Taylor, the commander, had orders to guard the bridge. Instead, perhaps thinking that he faced a mere raiding party, Taylor marched for Manassas Junction with three of his four regiments. It was a decision more courageous than wise.

The Confederates lounging near the junction were amazed to see a column of bluecoats blithely marching down the tracks as if on parade. They were so startled that they hesitated for a moment to open fire. For his part, Taylor first thought the troops sprawled out around the junction were fellow Federals and led his men right past several batteries of artillery. He was soon disillusioned, as the men down the tracks seized their muskets and opened fire on his column.

At that point Jackson, in an uncharacteristic gesture, rode out waving a handkerchief and calling on the Federals to surrender. A Federal rifleman drew a bead on him and fired. The bullet missed but ended Jackson's merciful urgings. The Federals were instantly caught in a point-blank cross fire between infantry and artillery. Taylor was mortally wounded, and the New Jersey Brigade fled in panic back to the Bull Run bridge. A. P. Hill pursued them, took great numbers of prisoners, and destroyed the span.

Late that afternoon, however, Ewell at Bristoe Station saw Federal troops in great strength approaching along the tracks from Warrenton Junction to the south. After a sharp skirmish, Ewell fell back as ordered to join Jackson's main body at Manassas. The Federals were closing in: It was time to go.

Jackson's men set fire to huge piles of supplies. Soon the night was bright from the flames, and a pillar of smoke was rising behind the withdrawing Confederates.

Jackson's next move turned out to be an astounding piece of deception. As planned, Lee was now heading for Thoroughfare Gap with Longstreet's wing of 30,000 men, following the same route Jackson had taken. Jackson had to hold out somehow until Lee arrived. For his temporary redoubt, Jackson chose Stony Ridge, a wooded hill seven miles from Manassas on the northern edge of the Bull Run battlefield of the year before. But his troops did not march there en masse. Jackson, it seems, issued vague marching orders, with the result that each of his three divisions took a different route to Stony Ridge. Taliaferro went directly to the objective; Ewell crossed Bull Run and moved northward; A. P. Hill took a wrong turn and went to Centreville, then doubled back. They would all meet at Stony Ridge, lie low, and wait for Lee. Accident or not, the three-pronged march would perfectly fulfill Jackson's own maxim: "Always mystify, mislead, and surprise the enemy if possible."

John Pope's army, scattered from the Rappahannock to Warrenton Junction, was ill prepared to respond to the Confederate challenge. Pope's original Army of Virginia remained the backbone of his force of 70,000, but it had been beset by problems. Morale in Banks's corps was at a low ebb. Sigel's corps was in better shape, but Pope considered Sigel so unreliable that he had put him under McDowell's direction. Pope also had two IX Corps divisions that Burnside had sent north from Fredericksburg under Major Generals Jesse Reno and Isaac Stevens, with Reno, the senior officer, in charge.

As for the reinforcements from the Army of the Potomac, it was no help to their orderly deployment that Pope and McClellan were at odds. Each had sent petulant messages demanding information of General in Chief Halleck, who equivocated in typical fashion. Pope assumed that when McClellan came up from the Peninsula, Halleck would take the field himself, with Pope heading one wing and McClellan the other. But Halleck showed no enthusiasm for that idea. McClellan, ordered to remain in Alexandria but to hurry his men and supplies to Pope, seemed to regard the whole campaign as a plot to discredit him and so did little to help. Many in Washington — including Lincoln — believed that McClellan wanted Pope to fail.

As reinforcements, Porter's V Corps and Heintzelman's III Corps had swelled Pope's army by 23,000 men. Pope soon decided that Heintzelman was but a lukewarm leader. He got on much better with Heintzelman's division commanders, "Fighting Joe" Hooker and the dashing Philip Kearny, who deemed McClellan nothing less than "a dirty, sneaking traitor." On the other hand, the V Corps commander, Fitz-John Porter, venerated McClellan and was openly contemptuous of Pope. Porter's intemperate remarks regarding his new chief ultimately would cost him heavily. Pope, for his part, greeted Porter with distrust: "He seemed to me to exhibit a listlessness and indifference."

Pope also faced resistance from Brigadier General Samuel D. Sturgis, who command-ed a reserve division posted near Alexandria. The hard-drinking Sturgis despised Pope and took no pains to conceal it. One night, when given an order that he assumed came from Pope, he snapped, "I don't care for John Pope one pinch of owl dung!"

Pope was at Warrenton Junction on the evening of August 26, attempting to bring some order to his command, when word came via telegraph of the attack on the Manassas supply depot. He suspected that it was just a small cavalry raid, but at 8:30 p.m. he ordered Heintzelman at Warrenton Junction to send a regiment up to Bristoe Station to see what was afoot. The regiment took a train to Bristoe, saw the enemy in force and hurried back to Warrenton Junction with the news. Now Pope began to concentrate his forces. He sent orders to McDowell and Sigel to shift from Warrenton north to Gainesville — through which, as it happened, Jackson had passed that morning.

Then at 7 a.m. on the 27th, Pope ordered Hooker's division to advance from Warrenton Junction and drive the Rebels off. It was Hooker's troops that met Ewell's Confederates at Bristoe that afternoon, prompting them to fade back toward Manassas. Pope himself reached Bristoe at dark, as the fighting ended; what he found there made it clear that he was facing not an isolated raid but Stonewall Jackson himself, with a sizable force. Pope was delighted, for now he saw the chance to destroy this formidable general once and for all and cripple Lee. Immediately he called up Porter's corps from Warrenton Junction along with the divisions of Kearny, Reno and Stevens from Greenwich.

Pope thought six divisions would be ample. He left McDowell and Sigel near Gainesville, and thus inadvertently, he had forces between Jackson and Lee. During the night, however, Pope let his enthusiasm for destroying Jackson run wild. He could not believe that Lee had divided his force as a strategy; surely, therefore, this audacious move by Jackson was no more than a large-scale raid prior to a full Confederate withdrawal to the Shenandoah Valley. That meant that the Rebels now would be desperate to escape back toward the mountains whence they had come — and all Pope need do is block that escape and finish them off.

At 9 p.m. on the 27th, therefore, he changed his orders: Now all his troops would converge on Manassas. His verbose messages fairly throbbed with enthusiasm. To Kearny: "At the very earliest blush of dawn, push forward." To Reno: "As you value success, be off at the earliest blush of dawn." To McDowell: "If you will march promptly and rapidly at the earliest dawn of day, we shall bag the whole crowd. Be expeditious and the day is our own." For all his zeal, Pope's plan contained a monumental flaw. By ordering McDowell and Sigel to Manassas, Pope was leaving Gainesville and the road from Thoroughfare Gap — Lee's route — uncovered. In his enthusiasm for whipping Jackson, John Pope had neglected to keep track of Lee and Longstreet and had no inkling of the approaching danger. "This," one of the generals opposing him said later, "is the order which lost Pope his campaign."

Back at Gainesville, McDowell had not forgotten Lee. McDowell was unpopular among the men, but not without some military skills. On August 26, Brigadier General John Buford's cavalry, stationed west of Thoroughfare Gap, had clashed with the vanguard of a large Confederate force. Buford immediately sent word to McDowell

at Gainesville that Lee, with Longstreet's wing, was moving along the same road Jackson had taken. McDowell decided on his own to put men in Thoroughfare Gap to block the Confederates' advance.

When Pope's order came to move on Manassas, McDowell complied, sending Sigel's corps and two of his own divisions. But he stretched his authority and sent his third division, under Brigadier General James Ricketts, to occupy the gap.

That night, the 27th, Pope at Bristoe Station could see the sky glowing red over Manassas; he was sure his enemy would be there for his dawn attack. He impatiently roused his staff before sunrise. "The General sat smoking his cigar and listening for the opening sounds of the battle," wrote Lieutenant Colonel David H. Strother.

Soldiers of Pope's Army of Virginia trudge north toward Manassas in an effort to evade a flanking maneuver by Stonewall Jackson. Though Pope believed that "the prospect of crushing Jackson was certainly excellent," his troops were not so avid. "This marching, sleeping on the ground without blankets and starving," wrote one soldier, "is beginning to tell very severely."

But it was nearly noon before the Federal troops entered the smoking ruins at Manassas Junction. The Confederates were gone. The Union soldiers, many of whom had been living themselves on green corn and apples, wandered about stunned at the sight of their pillaged supplies strewn about in such profusion. "As far as the eye could reach," noted Strother, "the plain was covered with boxes, barrels, cans, cooking utensils, saddles, sabres, muskets and military equipment generally; hard-bread and cornpones, meat, salt and fresh, beans, blankets, clothes, shoes and hats, from brand new articles just from the original packages to the scarcely recognizable exuviae of the rebels, who had made use of the opportunity to refresh their toilets." Then came a report: A large Confederate force — A. P. Hill's men, destined for

Stony Ridge but now off track — had crossed Bull Run and was in Centreville. Pope assumed that Jackson was now between the Federal army and Washington — a perilous situation. Impulsively, Pope now started his entire army toward Centreville.

Pope's soldiers had been marching hard for days; the supply wagons had lagged far behind, food supplies had run short, camps had been made without tents. "Tramp, tramp, tramp, eyes seeing nothing, feet moving only by habit," Captain Charles Walcott of the 21st Massachusetts recorded. "Up again before dawn, a paltry ration of hard bread given each man, and again, on." The men were exhausted, disgusted and confused. Walcott remembered his troops pushing along, "scorched by the noonday sun and almost stifled by dust, which lay ankle deep in the road, and sick at heart of General Pope and his strategy, which he had so bombastically told us was going to turn the tide of war in Virginia."

On the 28th, as Pope's army was shifting its sights toward Centreville, Longstreet's vanguard neared Thoroughfare Gap, pushing back Buford's Federal cavalry. Earlier a courier from Jackson had come through the gap and told Lee it was still open, with no sign of Federal infantry. Lee was relieved. A few men with a gun could make trouble there, and he could not afford delay; no matter how clever, Jackson could not hold out forever against an entire Federal army.

As it happened, however, that lone division under Ricketts that McDowell had sent reached Thoroughfare Gap a few minutes before Longstreet's advance elements. The Confederates found regiments and batteries awaiting them. This, remarked Long-

street, "placed us in a desperate situation."

Lee coolly rode to a knoll, raised his binoculars and studied the terrain, then issued his orders and went off to accept a dinner invitation from a country squire nearby.

Lee sent one of Longstreet's divisions through a rugged defile 5 miles to the north of Thoroughfare Gap, but that route was too rough for the whole army. He told Hood to dispatch a brigade to scale one of the peaks overlooking the pass, outflank the Union troops and attack them from behind. And he sent a couple of brigades up the mountain on either side of the road. This proved tough duty. The men clawed painfully up the steep slopes under the musket fire of Federal skirmishers and the blasts of canister.

Meanwhile, Colonel Evander M. Law, leading the brigade assigned to outflank the Federals, lost touch with his guide. "Letting him go, I moved on through the tangled woods and huge rocks until the crest was reached," Law wrote later. "Here we were confronted by a natural wall of rock, which seemed impassable." They searched and found a crevice "several feet above our level, where the men could get through one at a time," each helping the next up.

As Law waited agonizingly for his men to negotiate this passage singly, he heard cannon begin to thunder to the east, where Jackson's troops were waiting. Gradually the cannonade swelled to a roar; this was serious, much more than a skirmish. "Each gun sounded like a call for help," Law said. Help, indeed, was needed.

All that day McDowell's forces had been marching, first toward Manassas and then toward Centreville — where no Confederates awaited. One by one, the Federal brigades had moved out of Gainesville until the town was left unguarded. McDowell himself set out to find Pope with a few staff officers. He arrived at Manassas to discover that Pope had departed. Then McDowell attempted a shortcut to Centreville, wandered into deep woods and, incredibly, became completely lost. And lost he would spend the night, oblivious to all that was happening.

Georgia troops under General Longstreet battle a Federal force blocking the Confederate advance through Thoroughfare Gap in the Bull Run Mountains on August 28.

The last division to leave Gainesville was that of Brigadier General Rufus King, who had had an epileptic seizure the day before and whose haggard face, said an officer of the 24th New York, "showed that his illness was aggravated every day by the killing work." King's 4th Brigade had about 2,100 men, all from the West. The 2nd Wisconsin had seen a little action, but the 6th and 7th Wisconsin and the 19th Indiana were "strawfoots" — rookies — to a man. They were supported, though, by Regular Army gunners — Battery B of the 4th U.S. Artillery.

The commander of the 4th Brigade was a 35-year-old West Pointer named John Gib-

Steele Williams and his boy Walter, who fought with the 11th Pennsylvania at Thoroughfare Gap, were one of many father-and-son teams that served during the War. The elder Williams, a sergeant in Company F, was later wounded and discharged; Walter, who had enlisted as a musician, became a company sergeant just before the War ended.

bon, a lean, sharp-nosed North Carolinian with three brothers in gray uniform. Gibbon had jumped to brigadier general from Regular Army captain and command of the same Battery B that now was part of his brigade. He had been sorry to leave artillery for infantry, Regulars for volunteers, but he found that with discipline and drill these men from the West could be turned into crackerjack troops. Understanding soldiers, he outfitted his men in distinctive Regular Army black broad-brimmed hats. Veterans called Gibbon's men bandbox soldiers. But they were proud to be known as the Black Hat Brigade, and they could not wait to get into action and prove themselves.

By the time Gibbon's brigade set out late that afternoon, half of McDowell's corps — a division under Brigadier General John Reynolds — had already turned off toward Manassas. But then the orders were changed, and King's division made directly for Centreville. Gibbon marched in the middle of the column, following Hatch's brigade along the string-straight, dusty Warrenton Turnpike. It was about 6 p.m. and the sun was descending over the Bull Run Mountains. Four miles ahead of Gibbon's marching men was the Stone Bridge over Bull Run. On a nearby hill — within easy musket range of the Federals if anyone had cared — a horseman appeared. A Confederate cavalryman, perhaps. He watched Gibbon's men for a time and then turned and galloped away.

What none of the Federal marchers could have imagined was that this horseman was none other than the wily General Jackson himself, the object of their search and of Pope's frantic scurrying.

Jackson's three-pronged march from Manassas Junction that so befuddled Pope had come to a successful end. By midafternoon of the 28th, all three columns had reunited in a perfect hideaway on the old Bull Run battlefield. The masses of men were huddled in woods on the southern slope of Stony Ridge, which ran roughly parallel to the road to Centreville. In front of Jackson's position and parallel to the ridge was the cut and leveled grade of a rail bed on which tracks had yet to be laid. The hump of the grade made a perfect natural breastwork.

"The men were packed like herring in a barrel," wrote Captain Blackford. "There was scarce room enough to ride between the long rows of stacked arms, with the men stretched out on the ground between them, laughing and playing cards in all the careless merriment of troops confident in themselves, their cause and their leader. The woods sounded like the hum of a beehive in the warm sunshine of the August day."

Upon reaching Stony Ridge, Jackson had slept a few hours on what Brigadier General Taliaferro called "the shady side of an old-fashioned worm fence" before riding up on the ridge in plain view of the road. Shortly, one of his cavalry patrols captured a courier whose messages revealed Pope's earlier orders for the concentration on Manassas. That made Jackson suspect that Pope was moving to take up a defensive position north of Bull Run where he could be reinforced by troops from Washington. Jackson decided it was time to reveal himself, to sting Pope before the Federals got too strong. He rode up and down the ridge, nervous and irritable, "cross as a bear," Blackford said.

Jackson had seen Sigel's and Reynold's columns turn off toward Manassas. But then King's division came straight on, marching down the pike below the ridge on the way to Centreville. A brigade passed and another appeared, artillery in the rear. It was time.

Blackford, with a group of officers who watched from a distance, recalled the moment: "General Jackson pulled up suddenly, wheeled and galloped toward us. 'Here he comes, by God,' said several, and Jackson rode up to the assembled group as calm as a May morning and, touching his hat in military salute, said in as soft a voice as if he had been talking to a friend in ordinary conversation, 'Bring up your men, gentlemen!' Every officer whirled around and scurried back to the woods at full gallop. The men had been watching their officers with as much interest as they had been watching Jackson and when they wheeled and dashed towards them they knew what it meant, and from the woods arose a hoarse roar like that from cages of wild beasts at the scent of blood."

On the pike Gibbon's troops had been marching drowsily and unsuspecting in the quiet summer evening. "My horse and I were just wide awake enough to keep in the beaten road," an officer said. In the 6th Wisconsin someone had expressed a fear typical of the novice soldier: "I tell you, this damned war will be over and we will never get in a battle."

Gibbon was riding with his staff at the head of the column. Hatch's brigade had disappeared over a rise ahead of him. Those of Brigadier Generals Marsena Patrick and Abner Doubleday were out of sight behind. Gibbon saw several columns of horsemen come out of the woods; roving cavalry, he thought. Then Gibbon watched the lead horses swing left in unison and his artilleryman's eye recognized the move instantly: guns going into battery.

Gibbon ordered up Battery B. Commands

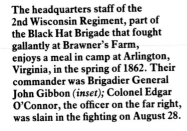

The headquarters staff of the 2nd Wisconsin Regiment, part of the Black Hat Brigade that fought gallantly at Brawner's Farm, enjoys a meal in camp at Arlington, Virginia, in the spring of 1862. Their commander was Brigadier General John Gibbon (*inset*); Colonel Edgar O'Connor, the officer on the far right, was slain in the fighting on August 28.

were echoed up and down the line. Gibbon surmised that he was facing light artillery attached to cavalry, one of Jeb Stuart's favorite harassments. A line of infantry skirmishers, spread out so they offered no target, would drive the Rebels off.

On the slope of the ridge, just above Gibbon's troops, was a tidy little farm — a house, an orchard and an old worm fence — where one John Brawner tended crops. Gibbon ordered the 2nd Wisconsin and the 19th Indiana into skirmish line and joined them himself as they started up through a field of broom sedge toward Brawner's Farm.

Blackford was watching from a vantage point above, and soon after Jackson's order to attack, he saw the Confederates move forward. "Long columns of glittering brigades,

like huge serpents, glided out upon the open field," Blackford wrote. "Then all advanced in as perfect order as if they had been on parade, their bayonets sparkling in the light of the setting sun and their red battle flags dancing gayly in the breeze." Six Confederate brigades, numbering about 6,200 men, were descending upon Gibbon's 2,100.

The Union men coming up the slope saw the enemy emerge suddenly from the woods with their bright, snapping flags and deliver a volley from a mere 75 yards. It was a devastating attack, and Gibbon's green troops might well have run. Instead, they held. Those who were still standing in line fired, loaded and fired again. On the road below, said Major Rufus Dawes of the 6th Wisconsin, "we heard the awful crash of musketry

and we knew there was serious work ahead."

Gibbon was now aware that he faced more than a mere cavalry skirmish. Suspecting that he confronted the army Pope had been seeking for days, he ordered up his other two regiments and sent couriers off to King and the rest of the brigade commanders.

The 6th Wisconsin then started forward. "Through the battle smoke into which we were advancing," said Dawes, "I could see a blood red sun sinking behind the hills." The 7th Wisconsin came up too. The Confeder-

ate line fell back a few paces, then rallied and recovered its ground.

Both sides settled down to wage a close, bloody fight. Two lines, Federal and Confederate, stood 75 yards from each other and fired as fast as they could load and aim. Neither side retreated, neither advanced. They took no cover, but fought by the book, standing there for an hour and a half, slaying each other in great numbers as the light slowly faded until the survivors on both sides were aiming at muzzle flashes.

Pennsylvania artillerymen near Brawner's Farm fire over a Federal skirmish line stretched across the Warrenton Turnpike on August 28. From cover in the trees beyond the field, Stonewall Jackson's troops return fire, raising billows of smoke.

"They stood as immovable as the painted heroes in a battle-piece," said Taliaferro, who was wounded three times in this fight. "Out in the sunlight, in the dying daylight, and under the stars they stood, and although they could not advance, they would not retire. There was some discipline in this but there was much more of true valor."

On Taliaferro's side, the 15th Alabama of Trimble's brigade found itself behind a rail fence on Brawner's Farm. "The fire from the Yankees literally tore the old rotten fence into fragments," Private McClendon remembered. "My position was in the immediate rear of Alonzo Watson. We were both on our knees, he firing through a crack and I firing over the top of the fence. I stood as high on my knees as possible in order to rest my gun on the top rail; my left elbow was at one time resting on his shoulder when all at once I heard a thud and felt a jar and poor 'Lonzo began to relax and sink, exclaiming in a low tone, 'Oh, Lordy, I am a dead man.' These were his last words but I didn't move but kept loading and firing."

The help Gibbon had sent for was slow in coming. Rufus King, the epileptic division commander, was growing increasingly ill and made no response. Patrick moved slowly. Hatch turned back, but too late to help. Doubleday alone responded promptly. One of the regiments he brought up to the battle was the 76th New York. It was green, and it knew a moment of panic when shells burst overhead. Colonel W. P. Wainwright rode among the men calling easily, "Oh, my boys, don't run, don't run. Think a moment how it would sound to say, 'the Seventy-sixth ran!'" One of his lieutenants said later that no pen could describe "the magic effect of those words." Then a mounted officer was shouting, "Come on! Quick! Quick!"

The 76th moved into a dangerous gap of a thousand feet that had developed between the 6th and 7th Wisconsin and stabilized the Federal line. The men of the Black Hat Brigade felt that the 76th had saved them.

Gun smoke now obscured the field as darkness came on. Major Dawes wrote: "During a few awful moments, I could see by the lurid light of the powder flashes the whole of both lines." Then, Dawes recorded, "our line on the left gradually fell back. It did not break but slowly gave ground, firing as savagely as ever." And yet, he added, the Rebels did not follow. Each side had run down. The 6th Wisconsin gave three cheers, but there was no response from the Confederate side. The night now was very dark, and there were no more musket flashes.

In the sudden silence the cries of the wounded rose in a low wail. The 21st New York, part of Patrick's brigade, had been moving toward the fighting — too late to join in. As it approached, the signs of battle appeared. J. Harrison Mills of the 21st New York recalled, "First a disabled battery, slowly hauling to the rear; then we begin to pass the ambulances with their moaning loads, and the sickening smell of blood steams up from the road. Groups of the slightly wounded come next, then bearers stooping under loaded stretchers upon which, mangled and distorted in agony, others are being carried to the surgeons."

Survivors went back looking for wounded friends. Some held lanterns high, but Confederate snipers fired on them and they continued the search in the dark. Surgeons set up field hospitals and the bone saws began to whine.

The next day, Blackford inspected the battle lines and later reported disconcerting evidence of the way both sides had stood and fought: "The bodies lay in so straight a line that they looked like troops lying down to rest. On each front the edge was sharply defined, while towards the rear of each it was less so, showing how men had staggered backward after receiving their death blow."

The casualties in this brief collision were appalling. "The best blood of Wisconsin and Indiana was poured out like water, and it was spilled for naught," Dawes wrote.

The Black Hat Brigade lost more than 900 of its 2,100 men, and Federal losses totaled around 1,300. The 2nd Wisconsin, which by the end of the War would have a higher percentage of its enrollment killed than any other Federal regiment, marched onto the field with 500 men and left 298 dead and wounded. The 7th Wisconsin and the 19th Indiana were nearly as hard hit, as were the two regiments from Doubleday's brigade. The 6th Wisconsin felt it was lucky to lose only 72 of 504 men engaged — almost 15 per cent.

On the Confederate side, losses were about the same, some 1,300. On both sides, the toll of officers was proportionately even higher than that of enlisted men. Two of Jackson's division commanders were wounded, Taliaferro and that talented fighting man, Richard Ewell, who lost a leg and was out of action for months.

Taliaferro wrote later that the fight at Brawner's Farm could be called a "drawn battle as a tribute due by either side to the gallantry of the other." For all its terrible losses, the Black Hat Brigade had gained, through gallantry and blood, invaluable seasoning for battles to come. Their transformation from green troops to true soldiers had been quickly accomplished. "The dust and blackness of battle were upon their clothes, and in their hair, and on their skin," Lieutenant Frank Haskell wrote of his comrades in the brigade, "but you saw none of these — you saw only their eyes and the shadows of the 'light of battle,' and the furrows plowed upon cheeks that were smooth a day before. I could not look upon them without tears, and could have hugged the necks of them all."

After the battle, Gibbon found King sitting before a campfire by the road. An aide later recalled the two officers' "anxious

Major General Richard Stoddard Ewell, Jackson's ablest division commander, paid a high price in the battle at Brawner's Farm for his love of joining the fight. As he led a regiment forward, the troops announced his arrival with a cheer that instantly drew a Federal volley. Ewell was struck by a ball that cost him a leg and put him out of the War for several months.

faces" in the firelight as they debated what to do next. Continuing to Centreville made little sense, since Jackson was here, but staying here was dangerous too. McDowell had disappeared, and no one knew where Pope was. Gibbon proposed withdrawing to Manassas and King concurred, even though an hour earlier he had told Reynolds that he would stand fast until that officer could bring up his division. After midnight, abandoning many of the seriously wounded, King's division marched for Manassas. Reynolds learned of this by chance and halted the march of his tired soldiers.

Earlier that evening, back at Thoroughfare Gap, Colonel Law's Confederates had fulfilled their mission. Slipping through the crevice above the pass, they had formed a skirmish line and descended on Ricketts' force from behind. The Federal gunners, finding themselves assailed from front and rear, had limbered their guns and retreated. By nightfall the pass was open, and after dinner Lee started his men through.

Ricketts marched back to Gainesville, looking for McDowell. Finding himself alone, he felt that his forces were much too weak to hold the town and so went on to Bristoe. Only Buford's tired cavalry remained in Gainesville to harass the Confederate advance. The way was open for Longstreet to march east to Jackson's aid.

In one more fateful error on the part of the Federal high command, Ricketts had neglected to alert McDowell or Pope about Longstreet's passage through the gap. In a few hours, then, Lee's army would be reunited — and poised for the crowning move of his great gamble.

Another Bull Run

"Forced marches, wakeful bivouacs, retreat, retreat. O, it was pitiful! The events of the past weeks are incredible. Disaster, pitiable, humiliating, contemptible!"

LIEUTENANT COLONEL WILDER DWIGHT, 2ND MASSACHUSETTS, U.S.A., WITH POPE'S ARMY

At his camp outside Centreville on the night of August 28, General John Pope was delighted by the distant rumble of guns from the vicinity of Groveton, four miles to the west. The fragmentary reports that came to him seemed to indicate a happy event — Stonewall Jackson was caught! All that remained was to pin down and destroy the enemy force. It seemed simple. General Irvin McDowell was approaching with 25,000 men from the west, or so Pope thought, while he had that many at Centreville. They would crush Jackson between them.

Pope harbored this fatal misconception into the early hours of the next day. He was sure Jackson was trying to retreat after what was only a large-scale raid. The idea that Jackson might be making a stand escaped Pope entirely, and in his excitement the Federal commander remained steadfastly ignorant of the approach of Lee and Longstreet. Worse, he was so preoccupied with trapping Jackson that he ignored his own army's need for provisions. When Commissary Captain David L. Smith reported to Pope that he had a trainload of rations at Bristoe available for the famished troops, the general snapped, "Return to your post. When I want rations I will send for them." For days his men had been marching far ahead of their supply wagons. Their fatigue and hunger would tell in the battle to come.

At 3 a.m. on August 29, Pope dispatched Lieutenant Colonel David H. Strother with orders to Fitz-John Porter at Bristoe Station.

Porter was to march his corps to Centreville. This, Pope believed, would trap Jackson in a vise between Porter to the east and McDowell to the west. On reaching Porter's tent, Strother recalled, "I found the handsome general lying on his cot covered with a blanket of imitation leopard skin." Porter read the message, dressed and went to breakfast. There, drafting instructions to his own subordinates, he glanced at Strother and asked, "How do you spell 'chaos'?"

Pope's pleasure evaporated when he discovered that McDowell seemed to have vanished into thin air; the general was nowhere to be found, and his corps was scattered in all directions. "God damn McDowell," he growled. "He's never where I want him."

The idea of crushing Jackson in a vise was lost along with McDowell, and Pope hastily redirected his nearest troops toward the scene of the recent fighting. The result was a series of piecemeal attacks on the morning of the 29th that never employed more than a small fraction of Federal strength.

Jackson's troops remained strongly posted behind the unfinished railroad grade, on a front 3,000 yards long. Attacks sputtered all along its length that morning, but they were concentrated on Jackson's left flank.

Under artillery fire in the center of the Confederate line, John Worsham of the 21st Virginia heard a loud thud beside him. "On looking around I saw a man at my side standing erect with his head off; a stream of blood squirting a foot or more from his neck."

This distinctive regimental banner was carried into the Second Battle of Bull Run by the 20th New York State Militia. Six standard-bearers were among the regiment's 279 casualties; another New York regiment — the 5th — suffered even heavier losses.

This was very disquieting, but what Worsham saw next was even more so — a new battle line forming off to the right, a little too far away for him to make out the uniforms. It grew longer, heavier and more ominous as regiment after regiment poured in. Was it a new Federal attack massing? Worsham's brigade commander sent out a courier, who galloped back shouting, "It is Longstreet."

The bulk of Longstreet's corps had passed through Thoroughfare Gap in the dark, slept a few hours and moved on at dawn. Hood's men led the march so rapidly that twice word came up from Longstreet to slow down. The troops were eager for the fray. They came through Haymarket in a cloud of red dust, went on to Gainesville and swung left on the Warrenton Turnpike toward the battlefield.

Lee was riding Traveller near the head of the column when Jeb Stuart galloped up.

"What of Jackson?" Lee asked.

"He has fallen back from Manassas and is holding the enemy at bay," replied Stuart. Then they must hurry, Lee said.

About 10:30 a.m. on the 29th, Longstreet's troops began filing into place on Jackson's right, and by noon the line was complete. It ran south from Jackson's position across the Warrenton Turnpike, its right end straddling the Manassas Gap Railroad. The whole Confederate line now was nearly four miles long, with four batteries of artillery on the high ground at the center.

Lee established his headquarters on a hill 200 yards south of the turnpike. He sat on a stump and listened to Jackson report while Longstreet rode out for a look around. A courier from Stuart reported more Federals off to the right beyond the railroad. The firing intensified on Jackson's front, and Lee wanted to march up and strike the Federal attackers on their flank.

"Hadn't we better move our line forward?" he said when Longstreet returned, preferring suggestion to command with his senior officers.

"I think not," said Longstreet. He did not like the lay of the land and wanted to know more about those Federals on the right. Longstreet was cautious by nature and preferred to let the enemy make the first move.

Stuart, meanwhile, had sent Captain William Blackford off to the right to examine the approaching Federals. Blackford recalled, "They were marching along a road grown up on the one side with high bushes and trees, and this together with the dust made it difficult to ascertain what they were." Blackford leveled his field glasses and saw "by the color of the trimmings on their uniforms that the flankers and skirmishers were infantry and not dismounted cavalry, and that there was a division or more."

Captain Blackford's report confirmed Longstreet's misgivings. To advance now would be to expose his own flank to attack. It was better to wait for the enemy to do something foolish. Lee mounted Traveller and went off to see for himself.

The Federals on Longstreet's flank consisted of Fitz-John Porter's corps plus Rufus King's division, now commanded by Brigadier General John P. Hatch, King having become too ill to go on. Porter had positioned Major General George Morell's division in the lead, followed by Brigadier General George Sykes and his Regulars. Morell spotted cavalry in the distance; he called a halt, threw out skirmishers and urged Porter to wait for the enemy to reveal himself.

Porter was digesting these developments when a confusing order from Pope arrived, addressed jointly to him and McDowell. They were to advance toward Gainesville. Pope, still oblivious to Lee's arrival, was ordering his generals to march right through Longstreet's position. The message, however, was so loosely worded that Porter and McDowell were left to do as they pleased.

McDowell, who had found his way out of the woods that morning, rode up to Porter about this time. He had a message from John Buford, the cavalry commander whose troopers had dogged Lee's advance. The dispatch had been written at 9:30 that morning: "Seventeen regiments, one battery and five hundred cavalry passed through Gainesville." Such a force could only be the other half of Lee's army arriving on the scene. This was certain notice of the dangerous turn of events. Incredibly, McDowell did not send word of Lee's arrival to Pope.

Gazing ahead, Porter said uneasily that he did not think he could advance without pro-

voking a battle. McDowell responded: "I thought that was what we came here for."

Still, McDowell agreed that moving toward Gainesville might be difficult. Instead, he took Hatch's division north to join Pope, who was coming up from Centreville. Porter remained where he was. Some of his skirmishers crept close enough to hear Confederates who were stripping a cornfield wonder out loud why the Yankees did not attack.

Pope reached the battlefield at noon and

Major General Irvin McDowell, whose army was soundly defeated at the first Battle of Bull Run, was scorned by men of both sides. A Federal officer captured at Second Bull Run was told by a Confederate guard, "When we see General McDowell in command of your troops, we regard it as being better for us than 30,000 reinforcements."

On the afternoon of August 29, troops of the Federal III and IX Corps attacked Stonewall Jackson's forces massed behind the embankment of the unfinished railroad. Cuvier Grover's Federal brigade temporarily broke Jackson's line, but Confederate reserves plugged the gap. South of the Warrenton Turnpike, Fitz-John Porter's V Corps remained inactive despite orders for him to attack the Confederate right.

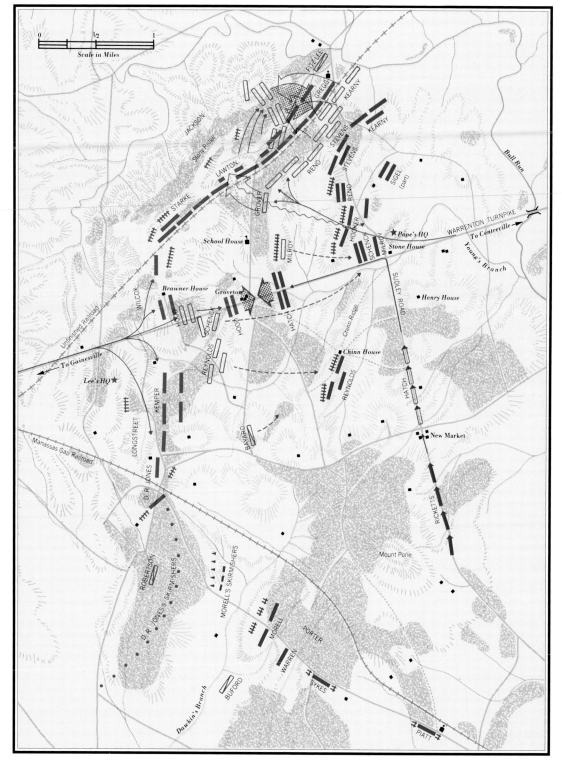

147

set up headquarters near the Stone House at the intersection of the Sudley road and the Warrenton Turnpike. Here on the Federal right, Franz Sigel's artillery was blazing away at Jackson's position. But whenever Sigel's infantry tried to advance against Jackson, they were repulsed.

Fresh troops — Heintzelman's 12,000-man corps and Reno's and Stevens' divisions, totaling 8,000 — came to Sigel's relief. But their attacks would remain uncoordinated and largely ineffective.

Shortly after 3 p.m., Brigadier General Cuvier Grover's brigade, part of Hooker's division, advanced on the Confederates. Grover's men moved forward through thick woods toward an enemy firmly established on the heights beyond the railroad grade. Martin A. Haynes of the 2nd New Hampshire recalled that "Grover rode the length of the line, telling the men they were to fire one volley, then rely upon the bayonet."

Emerging from the woods, the Federals fired and charged the railroad grade. As a wave of men started up the slope a Confederate volley tore through them, but quickly the survivors were over the top, shouting what one officer called "a wild hurrah." At the same time, several regiments found a gap in the embankment and poured through. It was too much for the defenders, and their first line broke. "Many of the enemy were bayonetted in their tracks," Grover wrote, "and others struck down by the butts of pieces." As Sergeant Frank Wasley of the 2nd New Hampshire moved forward, he stumbled over a fallen Confederate. Wasley snatched a huge knife from the man's belt and lunged.

"Oh, for God's sake," the Confederate cried, *"don't!"*

Late on the afternoon of August 29, Federal artillery moves into position to bombard a wooded area held by Confederate troops. Reports that the woods also harbored wounded of both sides were ignored. "As it was a point of great importance," one of General John Pope's staff officers recorded, "thirty pieces were brought to bear upon it."

Wasley's arm stopped in midstroke. "All right, Johnny!"

The Confederate first line was driven into the second; the second line shattered and fell back against the third. But now the Federals faltered. Grover's brigade was fighting alone, with no sign of support. The embattled Confederate third line rallied and turned on the thinned and exhausted attackers.

The 2nd New Hampshire held on, Haynes wrote, "until it found itself not only overwhelmed in front but flanked, and with rebels passing to its rear when the men made a break to escape capture." Back they tumbled, the Confederates closing in, and as the Federals recrossed the railroad grade they were exposed to a murderous fire of canister.

Eventually Grover's brigade was back where it had started. It had fought alone, as Federal units had all day, and like the others it had fought in vain. Of its 1,500 men, a total of 486 were dead, wounded or missing.

Grover's attack was followed by several more disjointed assaults by Hooker's and Reno's divisions. Then, about 5 p.m., Philip Kearny moved to the far right of the Federal position, having decided that there "I might drive the enemy by an unexpected attack through the woods." The one-armed Kearny rode along the Federal lines, reins in his sword hand, and roared, as a soldier of the 48th Pennsylvania remembered it, "Fall in here, you sons of bitches, and I'll make major generals of every one of you!"

Behind the railroad embankment on Jackson's far left, the South Carolina Brigade under Maxcy Gregg waited for the Federal advance. For Lieutenant Colonel Edward McCrady and his 1st South Carolina Regiment, it would be the sixth heavy attack they had faced that day. They were exhausted and their ammunition was depleted, and when the Federals pressed them, the South Carolinians gradually fell back to the top of a knoll 200 yards behind the railroad embankment. There they held. As the Federal attack waned, McCrady recalled, "we pressed them in our turn, and they broke and fell back."

Expecting another attack, one of A. P. Hill's staff officers approached Gregg: Could he hold out? Gregg was deaf and occasionally irascible, but withal, a great fighting man. Now he answered, according to one of his officers, that "he thought he could, adding as if casually, that his ammunition was about expended but he still had the bayonet." McCrady's South Carolinians were stripping cartridges from the wounded and dead of both sides. For they realized the danger: With their ammunition nearly spent they could be overrun, and then the Federals could turn Jackson's flank and roll him up.

Jackson's aide Henry Kyd Douglas wrote later, "It was a fearfully long day. For the first time in my life I understood what was meant by 'Joshua's sun standing still on Gideon,' for it would not go down. No one knows how much time can be crowded into an hour unless he has been under the fire of a desperate battle waiting for a turning or praying that the great red sun, blazing and motionless overhead, would go down."

Hard-pressed on the Confederate far left, A. P. Hill now sent Douglas to Jackson with a warning: Hill would do the best he could there, but he could hardly hope for success. The message, Douglas said, "seemed to deepen the shadow on Jackson's face."

Then Hill joined them. "General," Jackson said with a calm he may not have felt, "your men have done nobly; if you are attacked again you will beat the enemy back."

A volley of musketry erupted from Hill's front. "Here it comes," Hill said, spurring his horse.

Jackson shouted after him, "I'll expect you to beat them."

Gregg, indomitable, strode along the threatened line with his old curved sword from the Revolution, exclaiming, "Let us die here, my men, let us die here." Lieutenant Colonel McCrady remembered the scene: "We could hear the enemy advancing through brush and had not a round to greet them, but must meet the onslaught with only our bayonets. On they came."

Then there was a shout to the rear, and regiments from Virginia and North Carolina joined the South Carolinians. They charged forward en masse, some with empty pieces but all with fixed bayonets, rushing down the slope to crash into the attackers.

Presently, Douglas wrote, a staff officer rode up to Jackson. "General Hill presents his compliments and says the attack of the enemy was repulsed."

Jackson smiled, a rare expression. "Tell him I knew he would do it."

At 6:30 p.m., some five miles to the south, Fitz-John Porter belatedly received an order

These men of the 10th New York, also known as the National Zouaves, joined Pope's army after taking part in the Seven Days. Little of their colorful regalia survived the rigorous Peninsular Campaign; "We have been in misery indeed," one Zouave wrote, "knapsacks gone, and with hardly an overcoat, blanket or tent in the company."

General Fitz-John Porter, a staunch
friend of McClellan, made no secret
of his distaste for the commanders of
Pope's army. "Pope is a fool,
McDowell is a rascal and Halleck
has brains but not independence,"
he wrote in a letter to a friend.

from Pope drafted two hours earlier. "Your line of march brings you in on the enemy's right flank," Pope had written. "I desire you to push into action at once."

Porter pondered hard after reading this. It was all very well to advance, but what of the enemy troops that lay ahead? The sun was setting, and Porter's subordinate, General Morell, insisted that the hour was too late to move. In the end, Porter did nothing — and for this Pope would bring him to ruin.

Ironically, Lee was having no more success in persuading Longstreet to attack. Three times he urged an advance, and each time Longstreet demurred. Longstreet did agree to send out a division to probe the enemy position; he ordered Hood's troops to move east along the Warrenton Turnpike. Hatch's division of Federals, which McDowell had brought forward, met them near Groveton in a brutal little encounter that ended after the sun went down.

Though Hood held his ground that night, he knew he was in a poor position, and toward dawn Longstreet let him fall back. At about the same time, Jackson marched some of his units to the rear temporarily to replenish their ammunition. These movements would have a vivid effect on Pope.

The next day, August 30, dawned bright and clear with a promise of heat. Pope was up early in a blustering good mood, marred only by his anger at Porter's failure to advance the afternoon before. General John Gibbon, on a visit to headquarters that morning, found the commanding general and his staff sitting informally on hardtack boxes, Pope smoking a cigar and openly denouncing Porter. Pope believed that Porter wanted the campaign to fail so that McClellan would be called to the rescue. Petty as this seems, McClellan himself had given the idea some weight. He was at Alexandria with Franklin's VI Corps, Sumner's II Corps and a mountain of supplies that Pope's men now needed badly. Yet Franklin — presumably with McClellan's approval — had sent Pope an outrageous message: He would send a supply train only when Pope provided cavalry to escort it. "Such a letter," Pope said later, "when we were fighting the enemy and when Alexandria was full of troops, needs no comment."

But to Pope on the morning of the 30th, these hitches were soon to be made trivial by the sweeping victory he anticipated that day. At dawn he had received reports of Confederate troops marching west on the Warrenton pike. This was only Longstreet adjusting

151

his line and Jackson's units going back for ammunition. But Pope also heard that Confederate prisoners were talking about a retreat, and he concluded that everything had changed. "The enemy is retreating," he said firmly, and he began to organize a pursuit.

Pope had already decided to shift Porter to the north, unaware that Porter's force stood in the way of Longstreet's corps on the Federal left. Porter started to carry out his orders at 3 a.m., marching his men to the headquarters area at the intersection of the Sudley road and the Warrenton Turnpike. The only Federals now left facing Longstreet's corps were the men of a single division under Reynolds. Strangest of all the strange oversights of this day, Longstreet's 30,000 men remained undetected by the Union high command after nearly 24 hours on the scene.

Pope had a talent for ignoring what he did not wish to hear. Porter's report of a Confederate force in front of him was dismissed by Pope as an excuse to do nothing. Pope had by now received Buford's report of the 17 enemy regiments passing through Gainesville, but he dismissed it too. The clash between Hatch's men and Hood's Confederates at Groveton might have alerted him, but it did not. His only thought was to destroy the vanquished enemy before they got away.

Pope's plan called for McDowell to direct the pursuit. Porter's corps would move westward along the turnpike while James Ricketts' division, having arrived in the night from Bristoe, would push north then west along the Sudley Springs-Haymarket Road.

Strother carried the orders to Ricketts on the Federal right. "As I approached," Strother wrote, "I heard the angry 'zip' of bullets whistling by my ears, and when about a hundred yards off, the general called to me

to dismount or I would be picked off by the rebel sharp-shooters." Strother observed that Ricketts, upon reading Pope's orders, "seemed both surprised and annoyed. He told me that, far from retreating, the enemy was pressing him so heavily that he was not even sure of being able to maintain himself."

Pope received Ricketts' report in silence, and Strother asked if he should return to Ricketts with further orders. Pope, Strother noted, then "hesitated a moment and said, 'No, damn it. Let him go.' For some time after the general walked to and fro, smoking and anxiously considering the contradictory evidence."

Though Ricketts could make no headway on the right, Porter moved out with his corps and Hatch's division in the Federal center, just north of the turnpike. On the south side of the pike, John Reynolds' Pennsylvanians also began moving west — against the bulk of Longstreet's corps. At first the Pennsylvanians met little resistance. Then there was scattered fire ahead, and the lead regiment halted. Informed that the enemy was there in force, Reynolds snapped, "Impossible!" and galloped on. Then he reined up. Confederate troops were massed in front of him, muskets rising to fire. As he wheeled to escape, the orderly riding beside him was killed. Alarmed at the great number of Confederates, Reynolds spurred his horse through increasingly heavy artillery fire to warn Pope. Colonel George Ruggles, Pope's chief of staff, recalled the scene at headquarters around 1:30 p.m.: "Reynolds came dashing up, his horse covered with foam, threw himself out of the saddle and said, 'General Pope, the enemy is turning our left!' General Pope replied, 'Oh, I guess not.'"

Furious, Reynolds returned to his troops.

Confederate General James Longstreet was characterized by an Army comrade before the War as "a hearty, robust man overflowing with good spirits." But in January 1862 three of his children died of scarlet fever. Henceforth, noted one of his staff officers, "he was a changed man, very serious and reserved."

North of the turnpike, Porter's advancing columns began to take fire from Confederate skirmishers ahead of Jackson's line on the unfinished railroad. Even so, many Federal officers still concurred with Pope's analysis. Lieutenant Colonel Theodore Gates of the 20th New York Militia, part of Hatch's division, remembered "encountering several general officers who declared in exultant tones that the enemy was in full flight." A few minutes later the column jerked to a halt, under heavy fire. Jackson was still there.

General McDowell, with Reynolds south of the pike, seemed rattled, and now he made an extraordinary blunder: He ordered Reynolds, whom the enemy already had stopped south of the turnpike, to move to the north side to assist Porter. With Reynolds' departure, the Union left was virtually uncovered. One of the few Federal units remaining there was an artillery battery commanded by Lieutenant Charles Hazlett. Appalled, he called on a small brigade of only two regiments, the 5th and 10th New York. Their commander, Colonel Gouverneur K. Warren, responded at once, posting his men just south of Hazlett's six guns. About 1,000 New Yorkers now faced Longstreet's full might.

North of the pike, meanwhile, Captain Blackford watched from the Confederate lines as Porter's Federals, realizing that they faced an emplaced enemy beyond the railroad grade, shifted from column into line of battle and advanced again. "The march had scarce begun," Blackford wrote, "when little puffs of smoke appeared, dotting the field in rapid succession just over the heads of the men, and as the lines moved on, where each little puff had been lay a pile of bodies. But still the march continued with thinned but unshaken ranks until within pistol-shot of

Their ammunition exhausted, men of the Louisiana Brigade hurl rocks at Federal attackers from atop the embankment of the unfinished railroad. At right, troops from the 55th Virginia rush to the rescue.

our lines." Then, all along the railroad grade, a line of Confederates fired a withering volley. "Through a bursting cloud of light blue smoke gleamed a deadly flash of flame," recalled Blackford. "The first line of the attacking column looked as if it had been struck by a blast from a tempest and had been blown away."

Ten paces from a worm fence the color-bearer of the 21st New York went down. Another New Yorker seized the flag and fell with a bullet in his forehead. Then a third man took up the colors and was killed in turn. "I have almost reached a ditch," wrote Private J. Harrison Mills of the 21st, "when a stunning blow seems to tear me in two and I find myself doubled up on its dry bed. Like a dream in which minutes are ages, I dimly see the shifting changes of the fight. The ditch is deep with the wounded and dead, the living seek its shelter. Our Colonel, cool as on parade, walks along the edge."

On the Confederate side, Private Worsham of the 21st Virginia watched the destruction. "Their men were falling fast. Our

ammunition was failing, men were taking it from the boxes of dead and wounded comrades. The advance of the enemy continued. By this time they were at the bank; they were mounting it. Our men mounted too; some with bayonets fixed, some with large rocks in their hands." Several Federals were killed by stone-throwing Confederates.

Out of the smoke and frenzy, Major Andrew Barney of the 24th New York spurred his white horse atop the railroad embankment, waving his sword in defiance. It was a valiant but suicidal gesture. In tribute, some admiring Confederates cried out: "Don't kill him! Don't kill him." But Barney quickly fell, riddled by bullets. Soon Colonel William Baylor, commanding the Stonewall Brigade, led a counterattack, waving the flag he had taken from a fallen color-bearer. It was not long before Baylor, too, was killed.

South of the pike, Lee had held fire until the Federal attack was fully developed and fully vulnerable to the great force lying unsuspected on its flank. At last, Longstreet was ready. To Jackson's request for a divi-

154

sion, Longstreet replied smoothly, "Certainly, but before the division can reach him, that attack will be broken by artillery."

Eighteen guns commanded by Colonel Stephen D. Lee had been shelling the Federal lines to the north. Longstreet ordered four more guns to join them. "Almost immediately," he wrote later, "the wounded began to drop off Porter's ranks; the number seemed to increase with every shot; the masses began to waver. In ten or fifteen minutes it crumbled into disorder and turned towards the rear." Then at 4 p.m., Longstreet's 30,000 fresh troops started forward. Unopposed, they rapidly gained momentum.

Off in the distance, General Pope gaped in surprise as he watched line after line of enemy infantry advancing on his left flank with light artillery at the gallop. "For the first time in the campaign," said Strother, the general "showed strong excitement."

On the Federal far left, Colonel Warren's two lone New York regiments, the 5th and the 10th, braced to meet Longstreet's assault. Both were Zouave regiments. The men of the 10th were almost all in regular blue uniform, but the 5th wore Zouave gear — scarlet pantaloons with white leggings, blue jackets and red fezzes with yellow tassels. The 5th stood facing a woods; behind them the land sloped down to Young's Branch, a small creek with steep banks. Six companies of the 10th New York were posted in the woods as skirmishers, and the other four companies were to the left of the 5th.

The troops advancing on these Federals were men of the Texas Brigade, some of the best in the Confederate Army. As they surged forward into the dense woods, the 1st and 4th Texas veered off to the left; the other three regiments struck the New York skirmishers head on and drove them back.

In the moments they had to react, the skirmishers got off a few shots. Then the Texans were upon them, and many of the 10th's men went down. Those still on their feet rolled backward from the woods and into the waiting 5th. Frantically their fellow New Yorkers motioned them out of the way to clear the line of fire.

"There we stood like statues," said Private Andrew Coats of the 5th New York. "We could not see the enemy — but we saw streaks of smoke drifting between the trees." Then came the bullets, which sounded to Coats like "an immense flock of partridges," and the Federals started to drop. Private Alfred Davenport of the 5th remembered the sound of the bullets as "a continual hiss and sluck, the last sound telling that the bullet had gone into some man's body."

Once the men of the 10th had cleared their line, the soldiers of the 5th stood in their brilliant uniforms and fired a long, rattling volley. But the Texans rushed on, enfolding them until, as Coats recalled, "the right and left flanks of the enemy almost surrounded us. Where the regiment stood that day was the very vortex of Hell." Both color-bearers and seven of the eight men in the color guard were killed, but the cherished banners were saved.

Colonel Warren ordered the New Yorkers to fall back, but no one heard him in the noise. So they continued to stand and fight, taking terrible losses. A 4th Texas soldier, L. A. Daffan, reported that his regiment hit the Zouaves with "an enfilading fire which virtually wiped them off the face of the earth. I never could understand why this fine regiment would make the stand they did until nearly every one was killed."

General Robert E. Lee, accompanied by his staff, consults with General James Longstreet on August 30 prior to Longstreet's decisive assault on the Federal left. This painting and the one at right are small sections of a huge cyclorama of Second Bull Run painted in 1885 by the French artist Théophile Poilpot and a team of 12 assistants. Only photographs of the original work remain.

Lieutenant Colonel William Chapman (*on horseback at right*) leads his brigade of Regular Army men in a charge on the Confederate-held railroad embankment at Bull Run. "The slope was swept by a hurricane of death," a Federal survivor recalled, "and each minute seemed twenty hours long."

Joe Joskins of the 5th Texas saw the Zouaves fire a single volley. "The Texans didn't give them time to reload but with fixed bayonets moved upon them and getting within eight or ten paces emptied their guns at them — they couldn't stand but fled, we killing them at every step."

The recruits gave way first, and then the whole regiment broke and ran for their lives. Young's Branch "ran blood," said Private Joskins; Federals "completely dammed it up with their dead and dying bodies."

Private Davenport managed to cross the stream with bullets plucking at his clothes just after Colonel Warren's horse had leaped it in a single bound. Davenport thought of turning to fire at the Confederate officers, but one look back "was enough to let me know there was no time to stop." When at last the New Yorkers were beyond the onslaught and they rallied around Warren, only a pitiful few remained. The 5th New York had lost 297 of their 490 men; 173 were wounded or missing, while 124 were killed outright or died later of their wounds. The fatalities were the highest sustained by any infantry regiment in any Civil War battle.

On the hillside leading down to Young's Branch, a Texan recalled, the bodies of Zouaves in their colorful uniforms lay so close as to give "the appearance of a Texas hillside when carpeted in the spring by wild flowers of many hues and tints."

On swept the Texas Brigade, across Young's Branch and up the slope beyond. On the crest were the guns of Battery G, 1st Pennsylvania Artillery, commanded by Captain Mark Kerns. Panicked by the sight of the onrushing Confederates, the gunners ran for their lives. But Kerns remained and rammed home a charge of canister as the Confederates called on him to surrender. Instead he jerked the lanyard. At point-blank range, the charge tore scores of men to pieces. Immediately Kerns was shot down and his guns captured. As he lay dying, he said: "I promised to drive you back or die under my guns, and I have kept my word."

Despite its force, the Confederate advance was uneven, for on the left Jackson's tired men did not get moving until 6 p.m., two hours after Longstreet's onslaught. That meant that the Federals north of the turnpike were less hard-pressed. Troops there fell back in a little better order, and Pope began shifting to meet the surge on his left.

Hopelessly outnumbered, the 5th New York Zouaves confront a massive Confederate onslaught by Hood's Texas Brigade. In a matter of minutes, the Federal unit was virtually annihilated.

As the Federal defense of Chinn Ridge crumbles, infantrymen flee in panic, oblivious of their still-firing battery and the mounted officer trying to stem the rout. A soldier of the 88th Pennsylvania called the scene "a perfect bedlam."

He had two crucial points there below the pike. The first was a treeless plateau called Chinn Ridge. It lay about 500 yards behind the creek where Warren's New Yorkers had fought. East of Chinn Ridge, beyond the Sudley road, was a commanding rise surmounted by a pile of rubble — the remains of the Henry family home, destroyed during the battle here in 1861. Now Chinn Ridge and Henry House Hill became the keys to Union survival, for they controlled the route of retreat down the Warrenton Turnpike and across the Stone Bridge over Bull Run.

By 5:30 p.m., Colonel Nathaniel C. McLean's Ohio Brigade was already in desperate straits on Chinn Ridge, pressed from the front by South Carolinians under Brigadier General Nathan "Shanks" Evans and from the left by Brigadier General James L. Kemper's division. But fresh Federal troops — four brigades and a battery — were streaming south across the pike to come to McLean's aid.

Spearheading the Confederate assault on Chinn Ridge was a brigade of Virginians commanded by Colonel Montgomery D.

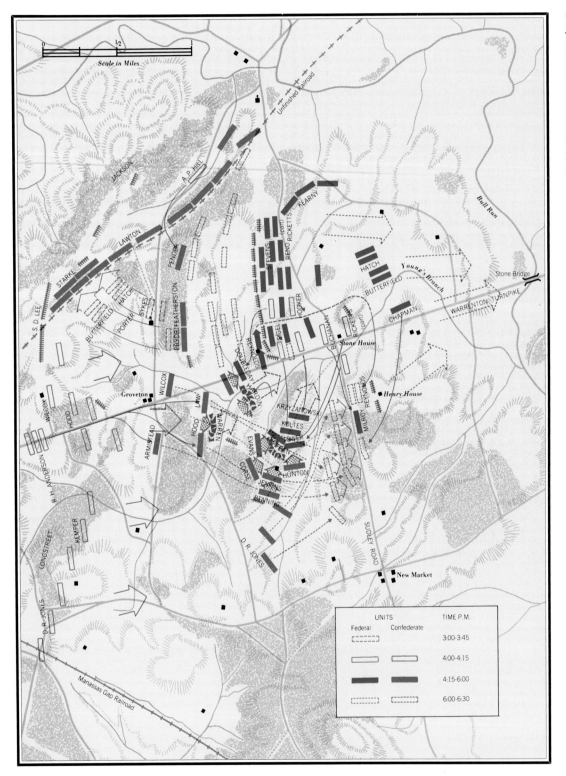

On the afternoon of August 30, James Longstreet launched a massive attack against the undermanned left flank of Pope's army. In fierce fighting on Chinn Ridge, the Federal brigades under Zealous Tower, Nathaniel McLean and Robert Milroy were eventually routed, but they gained enough time for Pope to establish a defense on Henry House Hill. North of the pike, Jackson began to push eastward toward Bull Run after repulsing determined Federal attacks.

Corse. Corse's men charged, wild and exalted, in a scene, said Private Alexander Hunter of the 17th Virginia, "which would make — were it not so terrible — a man love war and destruction for its noble excitement."

Hunter lost track of his unit when a friend was hit and died in his arms. As he started forward again, he saw two or three brigades of Federal soldiers counterattacking, their flags flying, bayonets fixed, lines well dressed. "At their front were the drummers beating the *pas de charge*, the first and the last time I ever heard the inspiring roll on the battlefield. I began to think it was time for me to get away from there — when I heard a shout — a savage yell from hundreds of throats — and I saw a brigade in gray coming at a terrific pace, the red cross shaking to and fro. Forming with them I kept on at the top of my speed — and the two opposing forces met in full career. A heavy volley on one side — a hurrah — a scream of rage. We got within ten yards of them — and they broke — and in a second they were running for the rear. Their guns were thrown away. They would unstrap their knapsacks as they ran — their hats would fly off — but nothing stopped them."

The Confederates paused to realign. Hunter asked the man next to him what was his regiment. "The 5th Texas," the soldier replied, "Hood's Brigade!" Ahead, about 600 yards away on the crest of Chinn Ridge, were the six guns of Captain George F. Leppien's 5th Maine Battery. Leppien's cannon blasted away at the foe down the ridge, flame flashing through clouds of smoke.

With a yell, the Virginians charged the guns alongside the Texans. Hunter recounted: "The veil of smoke had slowly lifted and we could see the muzzles of the guns —

their black & grim mouths pointed toward us. A horrid roar, then a shock that seemed to shake the very Earth. Then the dull thud of the balls as they tore their way through the bodies of the men — then the hiss of the grape — and the mingled screams of agony and rage. I looked around me. The ground was filled with the mangled dead and dying."

They dashed on with a great cry. Hunter wrote that "all order was forgotten, officers and privates were all together, each struggling to be foremost. The last definite thing I remember were those wild men in gray crowding up to the battery, some foaming at the mouth — they had run mad for the time. The struggle around the guns seems like a faint impression of a dream. And then I found myself seated astride a cannon — with the southern cross waving in triumph. Nothing was there but the flag with its handle rammed in the ground — and the lifeless forms of many of the gunners. The grass around the guns was burnt to a cinder."

In many such ferocious fights the Federal soldiers were pushed back. Clear across the great front that stretched on both sides of the turnpike, the Federals were in deep trouble. "The scene was terrible," said Sergeant William Dougherty, one of Sykes's Regulars. "Pope's whole line, pressed in front and on our flanks, was breaking into fragments and dissolving into a multitude of fugitives."

But flight was not total. The Black Hat Brigade, in the Federal center, did not waver. Troops on their left and right started for the rear, and as Major Rufus Dawes of the 6th Wisconsin remembered it, General Gibbon ran forward, pistol in hand, shouting, "Stop those stragglers! Make them fall in! Shoot them if they don't!" The Wisconsin

men showed their bayonets, but the retreat was an irresistible tide. Gibbon said he had no orders to go, so the Black Hats would stay. Yet Confederate sharpshooters had their range. Soon the beleaguered Black Hats saw that they were alone and realized that there would be no orders from above because no staff officer could reach them. Gibbon got the Wisconsin men on their feet and started them back. They had three quarters of a mile to go under fire before reaching cover, and they made it on the run in good order; Gibbon doffed his hat to them as they came in.

All thought of defeating the Confederates was now gone. The question was whether the Federal army could avoid annihilation. To do so it must hold the turnpike as far as Stone Bridge. Already, masses of guns, horses, ambulances, wagons and men were jamming a long stretch of the pike.

The situation, said Lieutenant Colonel Strother, "was awfully discouraging." He was returning after carrying orders from Pope to Heintzelman on the far right, but found it nearly impossible to move. "Organized regiments of infantry, full batteries and troops of cavalry in full retreat impeded my progress." When he returned to the hill where he had left Pope, it "was under a storm of fire and there was nothing in sight but one or two dead horses, solitary fugitives and a cavalry horse whose forefoot had been carried away by a cannon shot."

As Sykes's Regulars crossed the turnpike to move into position on Henry House Hill, Sergeant Dougherty happened to see the courageous Colonel Warren and 16 of his surviving Zouaves with their regimental colors. "Warren sat immobile on his horse, looking back at the battle as if paralyzed, while his handful of men, blackened with dust and smoke, stood under the colors silent as statues, gazing vacantly at the tumultuous concourse trudging by."

The five Federal brigades had been driven off Chinn Ridge by 6 p.m. But their stand had bought Pope time to strengthen his last line of defense, Henry House Hill. So far the Union had suffered a defeat but not quite a disaster; the Federals were being rolled back, but many continued to move in good order, making sure that the foe paid a price for their gains. Henry House Hill would tell if Pope's army would escape to fight again or lose everything.

Among the Federal commanders making a stand at the hill was Brigadier General Robert Milroy. Nearly hysterical with excitement, he led his brigade of Ohio and West Virginia troops onto a stretch of the Sudley road just west of Henry House Hill. Here the road was sunken, and it made a natural bulwark. He was soon joined by Reynolds' Pennsylvania division and a brigade of Sykes's Regulars. Meanwhile, Sykes's other two brigades and his artillery batteries were taking a position on the west

This panoramic view of the Second Battle of Bull Run was sketched by artist Edwin Forbes from the slope of Henry House Hill in midafternoon on August 30. On the ridge in the middle distance, Pope's front line, supported by masses of reserves, faces Jackson's Confederates on the wooded ridge beyond. At the foot of the hill is the Stone House (right), used as a Federal hospital.

slope of the hill, and Reno, with one of his brigades, was moving south across the turnpike to their rear. Pope and his staff were with Reno. All of them, Strother wrote, were "still under a bitter fire of artillery, the air shuddering with all the varied pandemoniac notes of shell, round shot, grape, rusty spikes and segments of railroad bars."

On and on rolled the Confederates. North of the turnpike, Jackson was gaining momentum, pushing Pope's right flank back toward Bull Run. "The ridges ran at right angles to the turnpike," recalled Confederate Colonel G. Moxley Sorrel, "and over these infantry and artillery poured in pursuit. The artillery would gallop furiously to the nearest ridge, limber to the front, deliver a few rounds until the enemy were out of range, and then gallop again to the next ridge."

As evening came on, rain clouds began to build. Strother recalled the sun setting "in a sea of fiery red clouds." A Federal soldier, watching the Confederates surge against the blood red sky, thought they "came on like demons emerging from the earth."

In the sunken road at the foot of Henry House Hill, Captain Theodore Lang of the

3rd West Virginia was studying the woods to his front when the defenders driven from Chinn Ridge "came rushing, panic stricken, out of the woods." Then the Confederates emerged, and Milroy's men opened fire, driving them back. "But the enemy," Lang wrote, "being reinforced from the masses in their rear, came on again and again, pouring in their advance a perfect hurricane of balls." A Federal battery on the hillside hurled a scathing fire at the enemy over the heads of the West Virginians, but the Confederates were undaunted. Their fire, Lang wrote, "grew more terrific every moment and soon the battery gave way, followed by a general stampede on our left, and shortly after, our own line began to show distrust and started by two's and three's to leave the line." Lang managed to hold his men briefly, but their ammunition was failing and no resupply could reach them. They began to withdraw.

Above them Sykes's Regulars, in position just below the hill's crest, blocked any Confederate move against the Warrenton Turnpike. Sergeant Dougherty reported that the Regulars "threw off their packs, pulled their cartridge boxes around to the front and knelt down in the grass to await the enemy. Some of the Pennsylvania Bucktail regiment came running up the hill, halted and fell in with our troops."

Meanwhile, General Reno led his old brigade to the crest of Henry House Hill. Captain Charles Walcott of the 21st Massachusetts recalled that "the white-haired General Milroy, who stood alone on the crest as we came up, was frantic with joy as he welcomed us; and as we dressed our lines, rode along our front, shouting like a crazy man." The Confederates below paused to reorganize, giving Reno time. He told Milroy to stop

163

interfering and then formed a strong line that curved along the rim. One of Sigel's brigades lined up behind Reno as a reserve.

About a half hour before sundown the Confederate batteries opened up on Henry House Hill with canister and shell. Sergeant Dougherty wrote: "They were so close that the sheet iron discs that held the tiers of canister were hurled through the treetops. The iron canister balls mowed the foliage from the branches and pelted against the trees and fences ominously."

Confederate skirmishers now appeared on Sykes's front, and his Regulars laid a devastating fire on the enemy. On the crest above, Reno's three regiments and a stray battery waited. To reach them, the Confederates would have to cross several hundred yards of open ground, moving up a gentle slope.

Reno, according to Captain Walcott, "walked along the line, ordering the men to lie down and keep perfect silence. We had not long to wait: the sun had set and it was beginning to grow dark when we heard a confused hum and the rush of many feet in our front; stand up was the order and every man was on his feet; the open space in our front was now alive with the rebel masses, and General Reno gave the welcome order, 'Give them about ten rounds, boys. Fire!' "

There was a thundering volley followed by very rapid fire; then it was quiet and the men lay on their pieces, listening to the cries of the Rebel wounded stretched before them. On the left, Virginians crawled up a creek choked with brush until they were facing the 51st New York on Reno's flank. It was nearly dark when the Confederates burst from cover with a wild yell. The New Yorkers whirled in dismay, and 85 of them were knocked down in a ferocious volley. But the 21st Massachusetts came swiftly to their aid, and in the dying light the New Englanders drove the Virginians down the hill.

A slow, dismal rain began around 8 p.m. as the last light of day vanished. The Confederate attack ended and the final Federal bastions still held, Reno's men on the ridge, Sykes's Regulars below. On the turnpike long skeins of Federal troops milled undisturbed, a staff officer at the Stone Bridge sorting them out and sending them across Bull Run to safety. Off to the Federal right, north of the pike, Gibbon's Black Hat Brigade had retired slowly, allowing the enemy to advance only with due caution. Seeing this excellent service, General McDowell paused and gave Gibbon and the Black Hats responsibility for the rear guard.

Presently, General Kearny reined up by Gibbon. His face was pale and his mustache quivered with anger.

"I suppose you appreciate the condition of affairs here, sir? It's another Bull Run, sir, it's another Bull Run!"

"Oh, I hope not quite as bad as that, General," Gibbon responded quietly.

"Perhaps not," Kearny replied. "Reno is keeping up the fight. He is not stampeded. I am not stampeded. You are not stampeded. That is about all, sir, my God, that's about all!"

The roads began to turn to mire in the rain, and exhausted, hungry, dispirited men who knew they had been badly led trudged through the mud toward Centreville. In the turmoil and darkness units were broken up, and all along the route of retreat officers stood by standards calling their regiments' numbers, gathering in the strays.

At his headquarters in Centreville, Pope tilted a chair against the wall, laced his hands

The defeated and downcast soldiers of Pope's army retreat across the Stone Bridge over Bull Run, heading toward Centreville and Washington. "This march was as tiring and disheartening as the battle," a Regular Army sergeant remarked.

behind his head and sat staring vacant-eyed at the room. A doctor watching through the window pitied him, but the more common reaction of his soldiers was summed up later by a regimental historian. Pope, he wrote, "had been kicked, cuffed, hustled about, knocked down, run over and trodden upon as rarely happens in the history of war. His communications had been cut; his headquarters pillaged; a corps had marched into his rear and had encamped at its ease upon the railroad by which he received his supplies; he had been beaten or foiled in every attempt he made to 'bag' those defiant intruders; and in the end he was glad to find a refuge in the entrenchments of Washington, from

which he had sallied forth, six weeks before, breathing out threatenings and slaughter."

Late that night Gibbon began the final withdrawal. By midnight all but a few stragglers were across Bull Run, and men of the 74th Pennsylvania destroyed the bridge so the Confederates could not use it.

A few miles away, by a fence-rail fire, Lee was receiving his officers' reports. Though Longstreet later lamented the lost opportunity to destroy Pope's army, the camp that night was buoyant. Lee wrote President Davis: "This Army today achieved on the plains of Manassas a signal victory."

Next day, as Confederate soldiers sorted out their losses and tried to deal with the

Death of a One-armed Warrior

As Pope's defeated army withdrew from Centreville to Fairfax Court House on the afternoon of September 1, a brief and bloody fight occurred that cost the Federals one of their few first-rate generals.

South of Little River Turnpike, near the estate known as Chantilly, troops from the Federal IX Corps moving east ran head on into a Confederate blocking force under Stonewall Jackson. Fighting in a torrential downpour, the Federals charged and at first broke the Confederate line. But then the Confederates regrouped, mounted a charge of their own and closed the gap.

With the clash in a stalemate, the fiery, one-armed Philip Kearny (*left*) galloped up leading a brigade. Without bothering to reconnoiter, Kearny threw his troops into battle, then started rounding up the scattered IX Corps men.

Kearny found the men of the 21st Massachusetts behind a fence at the edge of a cornfield. The general was in "an ungovernable rage," a soldier recalled. Pronouncing the field empty of Confederates, he ordered the regiment to advance. When an officer produced two captured Georgians as evidence that the cornfield was infested with the enemy, Kearny roared, "God damn you and your prisoners!" and spurred his black horse into the corn.

As rain fell and lightning flashed, Kearny came upon a shadowy group of soldiers. "What troops are these?" he demanded. "49th Georgia," came the reply. Kearny wheeled his horse to flee. "That's a Yankee officer!" someone shouted, while others cried, "Shoot him!" As the general galloped off, hanging over the side of his saddle Indian fashion, a dozen shots rang out. Kearny's clothes were torn, his saddle struck, and one bullet traversed his body from the base of the spine to the chest, killing him instantly. When the battle had again sputtered out, a group of Confederate officers gathered around the corpse. One of the officers later said, "I was conscious of a feeling of deep respect and great admiration for the brave soldier." And when Confederate General A. P. Hill saw the body of his prewar comrade in arms, he exclaimed, "Poor Kearny! He deserved a better death than that!"

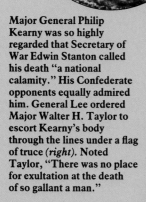

Major General Philip Kearny was so highly regarded that Secretary of War Edwin Stanton called his death "a national calamity." His Confederate opponents equally admired him. General Lee ordered Major Walter H. Taylor to escort Kearny's body through the lines under a flag of truce (*right*). Noted Taylor, "There was no place for exultation at the death of so gallant a man."

wounded of both sides, Lee planned his new strategy. Jackson would cross Bull Run to the north and swing around Centreville to cut Pope's line of retreat. But the muddy roads and the troops' exhaustion undid Lee's strategy. Jackson's march was slow, Pope dispatched a force to meet it, and the result was a brutal encounter in a driving rainstorm near an old mansion known as Chantilly. Two Federal generals were killed. One was IX Corps division commander Isaac Stevens, who died gallantly leading a charge and personally carrying the colors of his old regiment, the 79th New York. The other was the one-armed Philip Kearny, renowned for his reckless courage. Neither side could consider the action a victory, but the Federal soldiers stopped Jackson.

The Second Battle of Bull Run was over, another clear-cut defeat for the Union. Lost in the fighting between the Rappahannock and the Potomac were 14,462 Federals, more than 4,000 of whom were taken prisoner. Confederate losses totaled 9,474.

Pope was in full retreat to Washington. He tried to put a good face on things, but all he really wanted was to regroup behind the fortifications ringing the city. Lincoln, against the advice of his Cabinet, turned again to George McClellan, the only man whom the Army loved — the man, Lincoln once said sadly, who could do everything with the Army but lead it to victory. Pope was out.

Within the month John Pope was on his way to a new command in Minnesota. He would play no significant role again in the Civil War. He did mount a vindictive campaign to blame his loss at Second Bull Run on Porter's failure to advance on August 29. In that, at least, he succeeded. Fitz-John Porter was court-martialed and dismissed from the Army. For 20 years thereafter, the hapless Porter petitioned for a rehearing, and when he finally got it, he was vindicated.

On September 2, McClellan, yellow sash about his middle, mounted his great stallion, Dan Webster, and started for the Army of Virginia. On the road toward Centreville, as McClellan's big horse pranced, he met Pope and McDowell riding back in defeat. They paused for a moment and then heard the sound of artillery rumbling in the distance. Pope asked if the new field commander would object if he rode on to Washington. Not at all, said McClellan — but he himself would ride to the sound of firing.

Hatch's division happened to be marching behind Pope, and Hatch spurred forward in time to overhear the change of command. He hated Pope with a passion, and he immediately trotted back to his column and bellowed, "Boys, McClellan is in command of the Army again! Three cheers!" The division erupted in delight, and Pope rode away listening to his own men cheering his downfall.

For Robert E. Lee, Second Bull Run, known to Southerners as Second Manassas, was a triumph of generalship. Only three months before, his enemy had been at the doorstep of his own capital. Lee had taken a troubled army, reshaped it and then wielded it in a masterful display of strategy. Now he was at the doorstep of the enemy's capital. And Lee had no intentions of halting to maintain a static defense. He was, in fact, determined to maintain the momentum he had gained in taking the War to the Federals. Soon he would push farther north, all the way into Maryland, there to wage a decisive battle on a creek named Antietam.

The Price of Valor

"This may be my last letter, dear love. I shall not spare myself." So wrote Colonel Fletcher Webster of Massachusetts to his wife on the eve of the Second Battle of Bull Run. In the two days of savage fighting that followed, neither Webster nor the other officers pictured on these pages spared themselves: All were either killed or wounded. The Federals lost 699 officers, while the Confederates suffered a like toll in their higher ranks.

Many of those who perished were men of note. Webster was the only son of Senator Daniel Webster. Colonel John Means, who led a South Carolina regiment, was a former governor of that state. Lieutenant Samuel Fessenden's father was a Maine senator who later became Secretary of the Treasury. Colonel

George Pratt, who organized the first upstate New York regiment to leave for the War, was a prominent businessman.

Not all of those who fell deemed their sacrifice worthy. In a letter to his wife written as he lay dying, Colonel Thornton Brodhead of Michigan reproached his superiors for incompetence. "General Pope has been outwitted and McDowell is a traitor," he declared, and the remark was widely circulated by the Northern press. But even the prospect of death in a ruinous campaign could not dampen the dedication felt by most men. "Tell my wife she will never blush to be my widow," Lieutenant Colonel Joseph McLean of Pennsylvania begged a friend as he lay mortally wounded. "I die for my country and the old flag."

COLONEL THORNTON F. BRODHEAD
1st Michigan Cavalry, U.S.A.
Mortally wounded

COLONEL MONTGOMERY D. CORSE
Kemper's Division, C.S.A.
Wounded

COLONEL SAMUEL MCGOWAN
14th South Carolina, C.S.A.
Wounded

COLONEL JOHN A. KOLTES
73rd Pennsylvania, U.S.A.
Killed

CAPTAIN JOHN E. HAMES
18th South Carolina, C.S.A.
Killed

BRIGADIER GENERAL ROBERT C. SCHENCK
I Corps, Army of Virginia, U.S.A.
Wounded

BRIGADIER GENERAL MICAH JENKINS
Longstreet's Corps, C.S.A.
Wounded

LIEUTENANT COLONEL FREDERICK G. SKINNER
1st Virginia, C.S.A.
Wounded

LIEUTENANT COLONEL JOSEPH A. MCLEAN
88th Pennsylvania, U.S.A.
Killed

SECOND LIEUTENANT DAVID POTTS
26th Pennsylvania, U.S.A.
Killed

COLONEL FLETCHER WEBSTER
12th Massachusetts, U.S.A.
Killed

COLONEL JAMES M. GADBERRY
18th South Carolina, C.S.A.
Killed

COLONEL GEORGE W. PRATT
20th New York Militia, U.S.A.
Mortally wounded

LIEUTENANT W. JAMES KINCHLOE
49th Virginia, C.S.A.
Wounded

LIEUTENANT SAMUEL FESSENDEN
1st Maine Light Artillery, U.S.A.
Killed

COLONEL JEROME B. ROBERTSON
5th Texas, C.S.A.
Wounded

MAJOR DELAWARE KEMPER
Virginia Artillery, C.S.A.
Wounded

BRIGADIER GENERAL JOHN BUFORD
Cavalry Brigade, Army of Virginia, U.S.A.
Wounded

COLONEL JOHN H. MEANS
17th South Carolina, C.S.A.
Killed

LIEUTENANT COLONEL JOHN C. UPTON
5th Texas, C.S.A.

COLONEL J. FOSTER MARSHALL
1st South Carolina Rifles, C.S.A.

BRIGADIER GENERAL ZEALOUS B. TOWER
III Corps, Army of Virginia, U.S.A.

ACKNOWLEDGMENTS

The editors thank the following individuals and institutions for their help in the preparation of this volume:

Connecticut: Stamford — Don Troiani. Waterbury — Frederick W. Chesson.

Georgia: Tybee Island — Daniel W. Brown, Fort Pulaski National Monument.

Maryland: Smithsburg — Thomas Clemens.

New Jersey: Mystic Island — Fred Benz.

New York: Baldwin — Nick Picerno. Olivebridge — Seward R. Osborne.

North Carolina: Asheville — Paul A. Rockwell. Durham — W. J. Kenneth Rockwell.

Pennsylvania: Carlisle — Randy Hackenburg, Michael J. Winey, U.S. Army Military History Institute, Carlisle Barracks. Philadelphia — Karla J. Steffen, War Library and Museum of the Military Order of the Loyal Legion of the United States.

Virginia: Fredericksburg — Robert K. Krick, Fredericksburg and Spotsylvania National Military Park. Lexington — Robert C. Peniston, Lee Chapel Museum, Washington and Lee University. McLean — Mrs. Joseph F. Mullins Jr., Arlington House. Manassas — John Hennessy, Manassas National Battlefield Park. Reston — Thomas Bradley. Richmond — Cathy Carlson, Museum of the Confederacy; Sarah Shields, Valentine Museum; Rebecca Perrine, Virginia Historical Society; David L. Griffith, Virginia Museum; Mr. and Mrs. Carter Lee Refo. Stratford — Ralph Draughon Jr., Jessie Ball duPont Memorial Library, Stratford Hall Plantation. Sunset Hills — Robert E. Lee IV. Upperville — Lucy Brown, Mrs. William Hunter deButts.

Washington, D.C.: Eveline Nave, Photoduplication Department, Library of Congress; Feroline Burrage Higginson.

The index was prepared by Nicholas J. Anthony.

PICTURE CREDITS

The sources for the illustrations in this book are shown below. Credits for the illustrations from left to right are separated by semicolons; from top to bottom they are separated by dashes.

Cover: Painting by Charles Hoffbauer, courtesy Virginia Historical Society, Richmond, Virginia, photographed by Henry Groskinsky. 2, 3: Map by Peter McGinn. 9: Painting by James A. Elder on loan to Lee Chapel Museum, Washington and Lee University, Lexington, Virginia, photographed by Larry Sherer. 10, 11: Painting by Gilbert Stuart, courtesy Carter Lee Refo, photographed by Larry Sherer; Washington/Custis/Lee Collection, Washington and Lee University, Lexington, Virginia, photographed by Thomas C. Bradshaw II; from *Stratford Hall: The Great House of the Lees*, by Ethel Armes © 1936 by Garrett & Massie, Inc., Richmond, Virginia — courtesy Alexandria Library-Lloyd House. 12: Bottom, drawings by Robert E. Lee, duPont Library, Stratford Hall, photographed by Larry Sherer. 13: Painting by William Edward West, Washington/Custis/Lee Collection, Washington and Lee University, Lexington, Virginia, photographed by Thomas C. Bradshaw II. 14: Painting by William Edward West, Washington/Custis/Lee Collection, Washington and Lee University, Lexington, Virginia, photographed by Thomas C. Bradshaw II; courtesy Mrs. William Hunter deButts and the Virginia Historical Society, Richmond, Virginia — painting by B. J. Lossing, courtesy Arlington House, Robert E. Lee Memorial, National Park Service, photographed by Larry Sherer; courtesy Mrs. William Hunter deButts and the Virginia Historical Society, Richmond, Virginia. 15: From *The Face of Robert E. Lee in Life and Legend* © 1947 by Roy Meredith, published by Charles Scribner's Sons, New York — Arlington House, Robert E. Lee Memorial, National Park Service, photographed by Larry Sherer. 16, 17: Western Americana Collection, Beinecke Rare Book and Manuscript Library, Yale University, copied by Henry Groskinsky; drawing by H. Billings, courtesy American Heritage Picture Collection; Museum of the Confederacy, Richmond, Virginia. 18: I. N. Phelps Stokes Collection, The New York Public Library, Astor, Lenox and Tilden Foundations — National Park Service, photographed by Larry Sherer. 19: Painting by Robert Weir, courtesy Mrs. William Hunter deButts, photographed by Howard Allen. 20: Courtesy Frank & Marie-T. Wood Print Collections, Alexandria, Virginia — National Archives No. RG94-L69-AGO 1861. 21: Courtesy Mark Katz, Americana Image Gallery. 23: Chicago Historical Society Neg. No. I CHi-11622. 25: Painting by Cornelius Hankins, courtesy Virginia Historical Society, Richmond, Virginia, photographed by Henry Groskinsky. 26: Painting by William D. Washington, courtesy Virginia Museum of Fine Arts, on loan from Judge John DeHardit, photographed by Larry Sherer. 28, 29: Courtesy Frank & Marie-T. Wood Print Collections, Alexandria, Virginia. 30: Michigan Historical Collections, Bentley Historical Library, University of Michigan. 32: Map by Walter W. Roberts. 33: Museum of the Confederacy, Richmond, Virginia, copied by Larry Sherer. 34-39: Library of Congress. 40: Map by Walter W. Roberts. 42: Courtesy Ronn Palm. 43: Maryland Historical Society, Baltimore. 44, 45: Painting by W. T. Trego, courtesy Beverley R. Robinson Collections, United States Naval Academy Museum. 46: Valentine Museum, Richmond, Virginia. 47: Library of Congress. 49: Providence Public Library. 51, 53: Library of Congress. 54, 55: Minnesota Historical Society. 56-58: Library of Congress. 60, 61: Painting by Julian Scott, courtesy Union League Club, New York, photographed by Henry Groskinsky. 62: Library of Congress. 63: Courtesy Dr. W. J. Kenneth Rockwell, copied by Chip Henderson. 64, 65: Library of Congress. 66: Map by Walter W. Roberts. 67: Virginia State Library. 69: Painting by Alfred R. Waud, courtesy R. Gordon Barton, The Sporting Gallery, Inc., Middleburg, Virginia. 70: M. and M. Karolik Collection, courtesy Museum of Fine Arts, Boston. 73-81: Library of Congress. 82, 83: War Library and Museum, The Military Order of the Loyal Legion of the United States (MOLLUS), Philadelphia; National Archives Neg. No. 200S-WM-4. 84: War Library and Museum, MOLLUS — National Archives Neg. No. 200S-WM-12. 85: War Library and Museum, MOLLUS. 86, 87: War Library and Museum, MOLLUS: courtesy The New-York Historical Society, New York City (2); National Archives Neg. No. 200S-WM-25. 88: War Library and Museum, MOLLUS — The Historical Society of Pennsylvania. 89: National Archives Neg. No. 200S-WM-20. 91, 92: Library of Congress. 94: Courtesy Frank & Marie-T. Wood Print Collections, Alexandria, Virginia. 96, 97: Painting by Otto Sommer, Museum of Western Art, Denver, Colorado, courtesy Maxwell Galleries, Ltd., San Francisco, California. 98, 99: Drawing by Edwin Forbes, Library of Congress — from *The Photographic History of the Civil War*, Vol. 10, ed. Francis Trevelyan Miller © 1911 by Patriot Publishing Co., Springfield, Mass.; courtesy Michael J. McAfee. 100: Map by Walter W. Roberts. 102: From *Richard Snowden Andrews: A Memoir*, ed. Tunstall Smith, Baltimore, 1910; The Maryland Historical Society, Baltimore, gift of Charles Lee Andrews. 104, 105: Courtesy The New-York Historical Society, New York City. 106, 107: From *Battles and Leaders of the Civil War*, Vol. II, The Century Co., New York, 1887 — drawing by Edwin Forbes, Library of Congress. 108: M. and M. Karolik Collection, courtesy Museum of Fine Arts, Boston. 109-123: Library of Congress. 126, 127: Drawing by Alfred R. Waud, Library of Congress. 129: From *Battles and Leaders of the Civil War*, Vol. II, The Century Co., New York, 1887. 130, 131: Library of Congress, inset, from *The Union Cause in St. Louis in 1861*, by Robert J. Rombauer © 1909, St. Louis. 134, 135: Drawing by Edwin Forbes, Library of Congress. 136: From *From Manassas to Appomattox* by James Longstreet, © 1895 by J. B. Lippincott Company, Philadelphia. 137: Division of Archives and Manuscripts, Pennsylvania Historical and Museum Commission, copied by Robert Walch. 139: Division of Archives and Manuscripts, Pennsylvania Historical and Museum Commission, copied by Robert Walch; State Historical Society of Wisconsin. 140, 141: Drawing by Edwin Forbes, American Heritage Picture Collection. 143: Painting by J. P. Walker, courtesy Virginia Historical Society, photographed by Larry Sherer. 145: Division of Military and Naval Affairs, State of New York, photographed by Henry Groskinsky. 146: U.S. Army Military History Institute, copied by Robert Walch. 147: Map by Walter W. Roberts. 148: Courtesy The New-York Historical Society, New York City. 150, 151: Courtesy Dr. Thomas P. Sweeney; U.S. Army Military History Institute, copied by Robert Walch. 153: Courtesy Lee-Fendall House. 154: Drawing by R. T. Daniel, courtesy Museum of the Confederacy, photographed by Larry Sherer. 156, 157: Library of Congress. 158, 159: Drawings by Alfred R. Waud, Library of Congress. 160: Map by Walter W. Roberts. 162, 163: Drawing by Edwin Forbes, Library of Congress. 165: From *Battles and Leaders of the Civil War*, Vol. II, The Century Co., New York, 1887. 166: U.S. Army Military History Institute, copied by Robert Walch; painting by Julian Scott, courtesy Union League Club, New York, photographed by Paulus Leeser. 168: Courtesy C. Paul Loane — Library of Congress; Caroliniana Collection, University of South Carolina, copied by Charles E. Gay; Division of Archives and Manuscripts, Pennsylvania Historical and Museum Commission, copied by Robert Walch. 169: Museum of the Confederacy, Richmond, Virginia; National Archives Neg. No. 111-B-4383; Caroliniana Collection, University of South Carolina, copied by Charles E. Gay — Museum of the Confederacy, Richmond, Virginia; U.S. Army Military History Institute, Bonnie Yuhas Collection, copied by Robert Walch; Manassas National Battlefield Park, copied by Larry Sherer. 170: U.S. Army Military History Institute, copied by Robert Walch; Caroliniana Collection, University of South Carolina, copied by Charles E. Gay; courtesy Michael J. McAfee — Museum of the Confederacy, Richmond, Virginia; Maine State Archives Photo; Picture Group 5, Connecticut State Library, Archives, History and Genealogy Unit, copied by Gus Johnson. 171: Courtesy Bill Turner; U.S. Army Military History Institute, copied by Robert Walch; U.S. Army Military History Institute, Fitzhugh McMaster Collection, copied by Robert Walch — Texas Confederate Museum-United Daughters of the Confederacy, Austin, Texas, copied by Bill Malone; Caroliniana Collection, University of South Carolina, copied by Charles E. Gay; U.S. Army Military History Institute, copied by Robert Walch.

BIBLIOGRAPHY

Books

Alexander, E. P., *Military Memoirs of a Confederate*. Press of Morningside Bookshop, 1977.

Averell, William Woods, *Ten Years in the Saddle: The Memoir of William Woods Averell*. Ed. by Edward K. Eckert and Nicholas J. Amato. Presidio Press, 1978.

Baquet, Camille, *History of the First Brigade, New Jersey Volunteers, from 1861 to 1865*. MacCrelish & Quigley, State Printers, 1910.

Bates, Samuel P., *History of Pennsylvania Volunteers, 1861-5*, Vol. 1. B. Singerly, State Printer, 1869.

Blackford, W. W., *War Years with Jeb Stuart*. Charles Scribner's Sons, 1945.

Chamberlayne, Ham, *Ham Chamberlayne — Virginian*. Press of The Dietz Printing Co., Publishers, 1932.

Connelly, Thomas L., *The Marble Man: Robert E. Lee and His Image in American Society*. Alfred A. Knopf, 1977.

Cowtan, Charles W., *Services of the Tenth New York Volunteers (National Zouaves) in the War of the Rebellion*. Charles H. Ludwig, Publisher, 1882.

Dabney, R. L., *Life and Campaigns of Lieut.-Gen. Thomas J. Jackson*. Blelock & Co., 1866.

Davenport, Alfred, *Camp and Field Life of the Fifth New York Volunteer Infantry*. Dick and Fitzgerald, 1879.

Davis, Burke, *Jeb Stuart: The Last Cavalier*. Rinehart & Company, Inc., 1957.

Dawes, Rufus R., *Service with the Sixth Wisconsin Volunteers*. Ed. by Alan T. Nolan. State Historical Society of Wisconsin for Wisconsin Civil War Centennial Commission, 1962.

Douglas, Henry Kyd, *I Rode with Stonewall*. The University of North Carolina Press, 1968.

Dowdey, Clifford, *The Seven Days: The Emergence of Robert E. Lee*. The Fairfax Press, 1964.

Dwight, Wilder, *Life and Letters of Wilder Dwight*. Ticknor and Fields, 1868.

Fox, William F., *Regimental Losses in the American Civil War, 1861-1865*. Albany Publishing Company, 1889.

Freeman, Douglas Southall:
Lee's Lieutenants: A Study in Command, Vols. 1 and 2. Charles Scribner's Sons, 1942 and 1943.
R. E. Lee: A Biography, Vols. 1-4. Charles Scribner's Sons, 1934.

Gibbon, John, *Personal Recollections of the Civil War*. Press of Morningside Bookshop, 1978.

Gordon, George H., *Brook Farm to Cedar Mountain in the War of the Great Rebellion, 1861-62*. James R. Osgood and Company, 1883.

Gordon, John B., *Reminiscences of the Civil War*. Charles Scribner's Sons, 1903.

Hanson, Joseph Mills, *Bull Run Remembers . . .* National Capitol Publishers, Inc., 1961.

Hassler, William Woods, *A. P. Hill: Lee's Forgotten General*. The University of North Carolina Press, 1962.

Haynes, Martin A., *A History of the Second Regiment, New Hampshire Volunteer Infantry, in the War of the Rebellion*. Lakeport, 1896.

Henderson, G.F.R., *Stonewall Jackson and the American Civil War*, Vol. 2. Longmans, Green, and Co., 1909.

Horan, James D., *Timothy O'Sullivan: America's Forgotten Photographer*. Bonanza Books, 1966.

Horn, Stanley F., ed., *The Robert E. Lee Reader*. The Bobbs-Merrill Company, Inc., 1949.

Howard, McHenry, *Recollections of a Maryland Confederate Soldier and Staff Officer under Johnston, Jackson and Lee*. Press of Morningside Bookshop, 1975.

Johnson, Robert Underwood, and Clarence Clough Buel, eds., *Battles and Leaders of the Civil War*, Vols. 2 and 4. Thomas Yoseloff, Inc., 1956.

Jones, J. William, *Personal Reminiscences, Anecdotes, and Letters of Gen. Robert E. Lee*. D. Appleton and Company, 1874.

Kearny, Thomas, *General Philip Kearny: Battle Soldier of Five Wars*. G. P. Putnam's Sons, 1937.

Lattimore, Ralston B., ed., *The Story of Robert E. Lee*. Colortone Press, 1964.

Lee, Robert E., Jr., *Recollections and Letters of General Robert E. Lee*. Doubleday, Page & Company, 1924.

Long, A. L., *Memoirs of Robert E. Lee: His Military and Personal History*. J. M. Stoddart & Company, 1886.

Longstreet, James, *From Manassas to Appomattox: Memoirs of the Civil War in America*. Kraus Reprint, 1981.

McClellan, George B., *McClellan's Own Story: The War for the Union*. Charles L. Webster & Company, 1887.

McClellan, H. B., *I Rode with Jeb Stuart*. Kraus Reprint, 1981.

Marks, J. J., *The Peninsular Campaign in Virginia*. J. B. Lippincott & Co., 1864.

Marvin, Edwin E., *The Fifth Regiment Connecticut Volunteers*. Press of Wiley, Waterman & Eaton, 1889.

Meyers, Augustus, *Ten Years in the Ranks, U.S. Army*. Arno Press, 1979.

Michie, Peter Smith, *General McClellan*. D. Appleton and Company, 1901.

Mills, Charles J., *Through Blood and Fire: The Civil War Letters of Major Charles J. Mills, 1862-1865*. Ed. by Gregory A. Coco. Gregory A. Coco, 1982.

Moore, Edward A., *The Story of a Cannoneer under Stonewall Jackson*. The Neale Publishing Company, 1907.

Myers, William Starr, *A Study in Personality: General George Brinton McClellan*. D. Appleton-Century Company, 1934.

Naisawald, L. Van Loan, *Grape and Canister: The Story of the Field Artillery of the Army of the Potomac, 1861-1865*. Oxford University Press, 1960.

Nolan, Alan T., *The Iron Brigade: A Military History*. The Macmillan Company, 1961.

Patrick, Marsena Rudolph, *Inside Lincoln's Army: The Diary of Marsena Rudolph Patrick*. Ed. by David S. Sparks. Thomas Yoseloff, 1964.

Poague, William Thomas, *Gunner with Stonewall: Reminiscences of William Thomas Poague*. Ed. by Monroe F. Cockrell. McCowat-Mercer Press, Inc., 1957.

Regimental History Committee, Third Pennsylvania Cavalry Association, *History of the Third Pennsylvania Cavalry, Sixtieth Regiment Pennsylvania Volunteers, in the American Civil War, 1861-1865*. Franklin Printing Company, 1905.

Robertson, James I., Jr., *The Stonewall Brigade*. Louisiana State University Press, 1963.

Sanborn, Margaret, *Robert E. Lee: A Portrait, 1807-1861*. J. B. Lippincott Company, 1966.

Schenck, Martin, *Up Came Hill: The Story of the Light Division and Its Leaders*. The Stackpole Company, 1958.

Simpson, Harold B., *Hood's Texas Brigade: Lee's Grenadier Guard*. Texian Press, 1970.

Stern, Philip Van Doren, *Robert E. Lee: The Man and the Soldier*. Bonanza Books, 1963.

Strother, David Hunter, *A Virginia Yankee in the Civil War: The Diaries of David Hunter Strother*. Ed. by Cecil D. Eby, Jr. The University of North Carolina Press, 1961.

Townsend, George Alfred, *Rustics in Rebellion: A Yankee Reporter on the Road to Richmond, 1861-65*. The University of North Carolina Press, 1950.

United States War Department, *The War of the Rebellion: A Compilation of the Official Records of the Union and Confederate Armies*. Government Printing Office, 1902.

The Virginia Campaign of General Pope in 1862: Papers Read before the Military Historical Society of Massachusetts in 1876, 1877, and 1880, Vol. 2. Ticknor and Company, 1886.

Walcott, Charles F., *History of the Twenty-first Regiment Massachusetts Volunteers*. Houghton, Mifflin and Company, 1882.

Warner, Ezra J.:
Generals in Blue: Lives of the Union Commanders. Louisiana State University Press, 1964.
Generals in Gray: Lives of the Confederate Commanders. Louisiana State University Press, 1959.

Weld, Stephen Minot, *War Diary and Letters of Stephen Minot Weld*. Massachusetts Historical Society, 1979.

Williams, Kenneth P., *Lincoln Finds a General: A Military Study of the Civil War*, Vol. 1. The Macmillan Company, 1949.

Wise, Jennings Cropper, *The Long Arm of Lee: The History of the Artillery of the Army of Northern Virginia*. Oxford University Press, 1959.

Worsham, John H., *One of Jackson's Foot Cavalry*. Ed. by James I. Robertson, Jr., McCowat-Mercer Press, Inc., 1964.

Other Sources

Ackerman, Richard, Richard Ackerman Letters, Missouri Historical Society, St. Louis.

"Dedicatory Ceremonies Held on the Battlefield of Manassas or Second Bull Run, Virginia." Veteran Association of the Fifth Regiment of New York Volunteer Infantry. Eagle Press, 1907.

Dougherty, William E., "Eyewitness Account of Second Bull Run." *American History Illustrated*, December 1966.

Haight, Theron W., "King's Division: Fredericksburg to Manassas." *War Papers Read before the Commandery of the State of Wisconsin, Military Order of the Loyal Legion of the United States*, 1896. Burdick, Armitage & Allen, 1896.

Haskell, Frank A., Frank A. Haskell Papers, State Historical Society of Wisconsin, Madison.

Hopper, George C., "The Battle of Groveton; or, Second Bull Run." *War Papers Read before the Commandery of the State of Michigan, Military Order of the Loyal Legion of the United States*, Vol. 1. Winn & Hammond, 1893.

Hunter, Alexander, "Four Years in the Ranks." Unpublished manuscript, Virginia Historical Society, Richmond.

King, Charles, "Gainesville, 1862." *War Papers Read before the Commandery of the State of Wisconsin, Military Order of the Loyal Legion of the United States*, Vol. 3. Burdick & Allen, 1903.

Naisawald, L. Van Loan, "The Battle of Chantilly." *Civil War Times Illustrated*, June 1964.

"Painting the Peninsula: The War in Watercolors." *Civil War Times Illustrated*, December 1979.

Porter, Fitz-John, Fitz-John Porter Papers, Library of Congress, Washington, D.C.

Robins, Richard, "The Battles of Groveton and Second Bull Run." *Military Essays and Recollections: Papers Read before the Commandery of the State of Illinois, Military Order of the Loyal Legion of the United States*, Vol. 3. The Dial Press, 1899.

Stickley, E. E., "The Stonewall Brigade at Second Manassas." *Confederate Veteran*, May 1914.

INDEX

Time-Life Books Inc. offers a wide range of fine recordings, including a *Big Bands* series. For subscription information, call 1-800-621-7026, or write TIME-LIFE MUSIC, Time & Life Building, Chicago, Illinois 60611.